Subjective Atlas
of Amsterdam

Subjective Atlas
of Amsterdam

Edited by
Wouter Stroet
Anne Vera Veen
Annelys de Vet

ar c am

CONTENTS 4

Indira van 't Klooster, Anne Vera Veen, Annelys de Vet

A CALL FOR MORE VOICES

A call for more voices in the realm of urban development

I Amsterdam?
The marketing slogan has been our city's motto for years. But who is Amsterdam, really? Amsterdam still retains the image of an unprejudiced city, where everyone has the freedom to be who they want to be, to do what they want to do—yet inequality is on the rise.[1] The Amsterdam Centre for Inequality Studies defines the term as:

> a system-driven, environmental, or institutionally-formed difference in opportunity – that is, according to one's abilities – to fully participate in society and make use of the services that fully-fledged participation can provide.[2]

As an architecture centre, Arcam is concerned with the built environment. Not only a realm of historical and cultural importance, our architectural surroundings reflect deep inequality in countless ways. Construction and redevelopment are predominantly driven by invisibilised economic mechanisms instead of local need, resulting in office buildings, schools, homes, and public spaces that are out of touch. However, some structures of governance (democratic decision-making on one hand, and continuous participation processes, which operate with increasing difficulty, on the other) allow the public the chance to try to influence these developments. Thankfully, Amsterdammers—residents, designers, landscape architects, urban planners, activists, dreamers—possess powerful design tools. With these, they can provide a counter-movement against the economic dynamics that enhance and reproduce inequality, developing concrete solutions to positively influence the dynamics of the city. To make these changes inclusive and fair, it is essential to form a picture of Amsterdam and its inhabitants that is as rich and diverse as possible, keeping a wide range of needs, requirements, and complexities in mind. To this end, the conventional methods and information channels currently at hand are systematically lacking.

Usually, maps subconsciously represent that 'the world' can be mapped objectively and truthfully. But every graphical translation of spatial information, for any map, means coding: making choices, simplifying

1
See: Atlas van Afgehaakt Nederland | Kennisbank Openbaar Bestuur (kennisopenbaar bestuur.nl)

2
www.kenniscen trumongelijkheid. nl

realities, and omitting many layers of information. Which choices are made depends on the conditions under which a map is constructed. But what exactly does the cartographer know about a place? What kinds of human experiences are occurring there? Who or what is mapped, or not mapped, and why? As such, maps and atlases are not neutral, and they are certainly not objective.

This is why Arcam has invited Subjective Editions to jointly develop the *Subjective Atlas of Amsterdam*. The intention of our alternative mapping is not to provide a single answer or solution; this atlas deliberately presents a multiplicity of perspectives, through which the residents themselves have a voice—especially those voices that are often quietened. In collecting these perspectives, we have strived to be as transparent as possible about the terms, the process, and the intentions of making this atlas. The atlas' index ^{page 182} contains information about every contributing artist, descriptions of the local organisations who gathered them, and a timeline of our methodology and production.

The *Subjective Atlas of Amsterdam* gathers perspectives from beyond public consultation sessions and participatory processes for construction projects. The atlas shows a form of counter-mapping; surveying a place via a plurality of situated knowledges, local positions, and personal reflections. This allows the mapped information to reflect the different ways in which inhabitants comprehend a city, region, or place. This collaborative methodology recognises the importance of subjectivity and intuition in the production of knowledge. It challenges and embraces the social, political, and cultural circumstances of our everyday realities. This alone makes this publication an incredibly important tool for strengthening both accessibility to the city and justice within it.

This atlas would not have been possible without the commitment of seven diverse partners who expressed their enthusiasm to collaborate on such a project. Each is engaged with the city in a different way; either as members of a particular residential community, a social or cultural movement, an activist group, artists' collective, student group, a queer archive, or as inclusive urbanists. They organised workshops hosted at familiar locations, where they invited people to map the city in their own unique way. Each participant did so as a subjective individual with personal feelings and experiences, rather than as a representative of a larger group or exemplary category. Additionally, visitors to Arcam were invited to draw their own subjective map or flag and to hang them between other visual contributions on display. Page after page, inhabtants from all corners of Amsterdam have translated their observations and experiences into maps, drawings, photos, and graphics with generosity, imagination, and vision.

As facilitators of the process, we[3] allowed ourselves to be guided by the wishes, workflow, and rhythm of the participants—and the languages they spoke. During the work sessions, experiences were shared in *straattaal* (local slang), Dutch, English, Arabic, Turkish, and many more tongues. After navigating a multitude of experiences, visions, and voices, we chose to publish the atlas in the language that connected most people: English. Distilling their contributions into a single language serves to create space for both image and imagination.

As such, this atlas does not aspire to 'completeness'. Because after all, how would it be possible to capture the completeness of human experience in one publication? Instead, the array of contributions offers a snapshot of a city in which lives and experiences are ongoing. What is shared is sometimes entertaining, such as the amusing habit of Amsterdammers communicating their political views by placing stickers on traffic light poles [page 92]. Sometimes, the pages imbue a cosy, familiar feeling of Mokum,[4] the nickname of our beloved city [pages 126, 136, and 166]. But much more often, the personal experiences articulated are uncomfortable or painful. What does it say about Amsterdam if tap water is only free at the public water fountains in parks [page 84]? If a trans person is not safe in all areas of the city [page 158]? If there are mechanisms of exclusion that prevent sleeping in public spaces [page 82], promote housing insecurity [page 142], or lead to dirty streets [page 90]? Can we be proud of a city where refugees are systematically housed in the outskirts, instead of being welcome as part of vibrant urban life [page 120, 142]? A city where one can barely get around in

[3]
**Indira
van 't Klooster**
(Arcam, Director)

Anne Vera Veen
(Arcam, Visual
Anthropologist)

Annelys de Vet
(Subjective
Editions,
Editor-in-chief)

[4]
Mokum means
'city' in Yiddish,
stemming from a
time when Amsterdam's dialect included many words
from its once large
and thriving Jewish
population.

a wheelchair page 96? Where not everyone is represented, page 160 or where one's own history is ignored page 112?

This *Subjective Atlas of Amsterdam* is founded on the belief that designers, builders, developers, and policymakers have a responsibility to address and engage with social inequality. This is not something that happens naturally. First, there must be an understanding that the conversation about the 'built city' may not be exclusively held by professionals. The jargon that is spoken (sight lines, plan horizon, plinth), the processes that are established (participation, selection procedures), the channels by which the public are contacted (one-sided communication channels), and what designers are accustomed to accept as the result (a building, or area), are all part of a much larger whole; a process that must be widely inclusive.

Architects and designers will also have to reconsider the criteria for what constitutes quality, as used by aesthetics committees and supervisors or in architectural tenders. The preference for 'objectively' measurable criteria, such as 'square metres', 'compliance with Building Decree regulations', 'fitting the environment', or 'use of materials' leaves no room for social or cultural considerations from the perspective of the individual user of the city. This atlas shows that different knowledges emerge with different methods. It offers designers and policymakers a sample of starting points for making the city a better place for everyone, offering a method with which to search for nuanced realities in the future. The layered collection of experiences forms a plea for the presence of more voices; for polyphony in the spatial process. With that message in mind, Arcam will be visiting policymakers, selection panels, and drawing rooms in the city.

A lot of love for and devotion to Amsterdam can be felt throughout the atlas, despite the flaws that some contributions address. Above all, it shows us how committed the voices in this city are to making Amsterdam a welcoming, forgiving, compassionate, and inviting place. Wherever this is not currently the case, people are fighting to achieve it. In all its nuances, joy, and striving, this atlas is an ode to Amsterdam: a strong-willed city, adaptable to and for all of us.

Think big
and act small

Najah Aouaki is an independent economist and urban strategist. For more
than fifteen years she has been involved in various Amsterdam-based projects at the intersection of policy, economy, art, and society, including Bureau
Broedplaatsen, Westergasfabriek, Javakwartier, and the street-art project
R.U.A. in the H-buurt in Amsterdam Zuidoost. For each innovative project,
Najah approaches economy as a system that should serve our wellbeing,
while the human dimension and an equal playing field form the drivers of that
system. This perspective applies to her project on the Javastraat—a constantly changing, multiethnic street in the east of Amsterdam—which supports
existing retailers to be more visible, and subsequently more resilient, as the
district experiences gentrification. In the exhibition *Speculate or Die Tryin'*, she
combines the urban development and social history of another transitioning
Amsterdam neighbourhood, Zuidoost, with a plea to harness the potential of
the current community in future planning, instead of undermining it.

The atlas' editors, Annelys de Vet and Anne Vera Veen, admire her critical eye
and analytical way of working. In their conversation with Najah about the *Subjective Atlas* as a methodology, they begin the conversation with the question,
'How was your morning?' It was with this question they began each workshop
for the atlas, as a sort of icebreaker to get everyone talking on a personal level,
before engaging more deeply in certain topics together.

Najah Aouaki: I feel happy and good. Since the cast was removed from
my foot, I'm a bit more agile again. It's misty outside, and sitting inside,
I'm upset about a newspaper article stating that healthy food is more
expensive than unhealthy food. I think, 'why do we keep investigating
things that we already know?' At the same time, it is incredibly important
to continue to address these forms of unequal access to wellbeing.

> **What does this snapshot of your morning say about your view
> of the world as an economist?**

In these neoliberal times, we have reduced 'economics' to economic
growth, and people to rational, calculating beings in a money-making
system. But economics is fundamentally a much broader concept than
this: it is the doctrine on the distribution of scarce resources in order to

meet human needs. Seen in this way, the economy is not separate from the social domain and our wellbeing.

But now, economic growth is the starting point, where we assume that the masses automatically benefit from the wealth created; the trickle-down effect. I advocate for an economy that serves our wellbeing, where human aspirations and challenges are central, instead of maximising financial returns. We also sacrifice 'direction and control' if we concede too much power to market forces. What is currently lacking in the pursuit of diversity, outside this atlas, is attention to an increasing group of people who are less and less represented in our official frameworks and statistics. For example, does the term 'unemployed' also cover someone who hasn't had a job for ten years or longer?

Since the 1980s, Western cities like Amsterdam made the shift from an economy based on industrial production to an economy based on knowledge. To attract the needed, highly educated so-called knowledge workers, investments were made to provide for them: a well-known gentrification strategy. The labour class, however, was pushed back, both geographically (towards the outskirts of the city) and conceptually (not given attention). It became clear that access to basic services such as housing and public transport, or the right to a beautiful urban environment, are not available to all equally. We should be asking ourselves, for whom are we building the most beautiful buildings?

[5] Florentinus Marinus (Floor) Wibaut was alderman in Amsterdam between 1914 and 1931.

I am a fan of Floor Wibaut,[5] who believed everyone should be able to live in a nice environment and have a good life, despite their income. He created a municipal construction company in order to provide affordable housing —affordable and also of high quality, as he believed that good housing and a beautiful built environment would have a positive effect on quality of life and emancipation. After relying on the trickle-down effect for the last decades, we now need poverty alleviation. This is more about damage control than forward-looking strategy. We must return to a society that offers opportunities instead of relying on a trickle-down effect that doesn't exist. On the contrary, neoliberalism goes hand in hand with growing inequality.

How can the *Subjective Atlas* as a method contribute to the paradigms you just described?
The neoliberal discourse within which we have developed our cities over the past decades has put so much focus on pursuing economic growth that we have forgotten that cities house a society; that cities are a social construct, an ecosystem of intertwined communities. When we talk about urban development, we should acknowledge the importance of care networks, social connections, and access to nature, all aspects that contribute to people's wellbeing. That can be clearly seen in the *Subjective Atlas of Amsterdam*.

Are there entries in the *Subjective Atlas* that illustrate this?
The perspective of a subjective atlas is already enormously valuable; there is no standard. Whereas in the professional world of policy, construction, and design, the view is often much more one-sided. There seems to be an implicit standard that isn't questioned. People may not even be aware of that: how you value quality, how you view social interaction. This atlas shows that there is no obvious answer, and therefore no one standard. By demonstrating the differences between the professional and subjective methods, you draw people's attention to that fact. The example on page 78 shows that the *nieuwe Noorderlingen*[6] like to place a picnic table in front of their house in public space. Even though all neighbours are probably welcome to join them, this well-intentioned act of appropriating that space with a picnic table stands in contrast to the pre-existing activities that the sitting residents were engaging in in this public space. Having big gatherings where loud music is played, playing sports, having family barbecues, or just hanging around ... The new residents are not always aware that they are setting a new norm, or deviating from an old one. Subsequently, earlier residents who continue to use the grass how they always have done are then perceived as a nuisance. And finally, this new perception of public nuisance is upheld. New residents set new rules, and then let the old ones back in on those new terms. There is not only subjectivity in an experience; there is also subjectivity to be found in enforcement! Just look at benches designed specifically so one cannot lay or sleep on them page 82. Or to a man who names the OBA (public library),

[6] Newcomers to the neighbourhood of Amsterdam Noord, who moved in with the recent wave of gentrification.

the winter shelter, and World House as the first three places he got to know after arriving in Amsterdam, since these were the most accessible to him as a refugee, and the only places he could be like the rest, not a refugee.

What stands out to you about this *Subjective Atlas of Amsterdam*?
A clear choice has been made to let these specific people speak, those who are pushed into the margins. From my personal background, I support that because you are uncovering the complexities of spatial inequalities. I would additionally have included the perspectives of a broader range of people, to see the contrast even more sharply, and to make comparisons. Even then, you must remain aware of the question of whose field of vision you are actually broadening with this atlas. For some people, none of this is news. The atlas provides insight into what the city means to different people. By showing that, designers, developers, and policymakers will also realise that there are more realities out there, and that no standard should be implied. These multiple realities should be the beginning of dialogue about city-making. But in which reality this conversation is contextualised, and with which urgency all the different realities are included, makes a lot of difference. Many designers probably think they are already engaging users. But to what extent do they subconsciously take a certain viewpoint or show certain preferences? Even at the start of a participation process, many assumptions are already being made implicitly. Professionals in the design world often do not realise how many different people and needs have already been excluded before even beginning. Inclusion is not a checklist. This atlas offers the opportunity for everyone to question themselves again; in the way you view the world, the society you live in, the privileges you have, the way you work, and the selection of your team.

We are making this atlas partly as an invitation to designers and policymakers to adapt their practices accordingly. Are we thinking big enough?
I think we need to change the view of the economy as a money-machine to a view of the economy as a means of wellbeing, to offer as many people as possible a valuable living environment, where they can access basic

amenities, such as healthy food. That framework of wellbeing is also very relevant for architects! For Wibaut, the goal was to ensure quality housing for the working class. We need to get that mentality back, where the revenue model comes only after the preconditions for wellbeing have been established. That is a design challenge in and of itself. That is why it is not really fair to assign such a task to designers, because these decisive choices have already been made before they even get to work.

Changing the financial and economic frameworks is essential if we really want to develop our cities in an inclusive manner, and in a way that all inhabitants feel like they matter, not only those who have money to spend. Creating frameworks that truly allow for inclusivity and equality is the only path to better solutions. That also creates space for more benefits in the long run. Everything we invest in wellbeing now results in cost savings in the future, when it comes to health, quality of life, and maintenance. Look at the baby boom generation, for example, who benefited from the post-WWII policies and investments that created opportunities for the emancipation of the working class. Between World War II and the 1980s, there was a period when inequality dropped, only to rise again.

Currently, not only are resources for wellbeing being distributed very unevenly, but one's future increasingly depends on where someone was born. Segregation and inequality are on the rise. We need to usher in a different discourse to enable a new future. There are enough methods, we just need to claim the space. Think of concepts like The 15-Minute City or the Just City Index.[7] It's about thinking big and acting small. The framework of wellbeing is the grand vision of the distribution of money and resources, space and beauty. But city-making also requires microsurgical work, ensuring that at every level, you can both serve and reach everyone. We shouldn't talk about inclusive solutions. We really need a completely different framework!

7
The 15-Minute City is a residential urban concept in which most daily necessities and services should be located within a 15-minute walk or bike ride from any point in the city. The Just City Index is a framework of fifty values, to be used as a tool for communities to establish their own definition and principles for what makes each city more just.

Galaxy Amsterdam with exclusive access
Elke

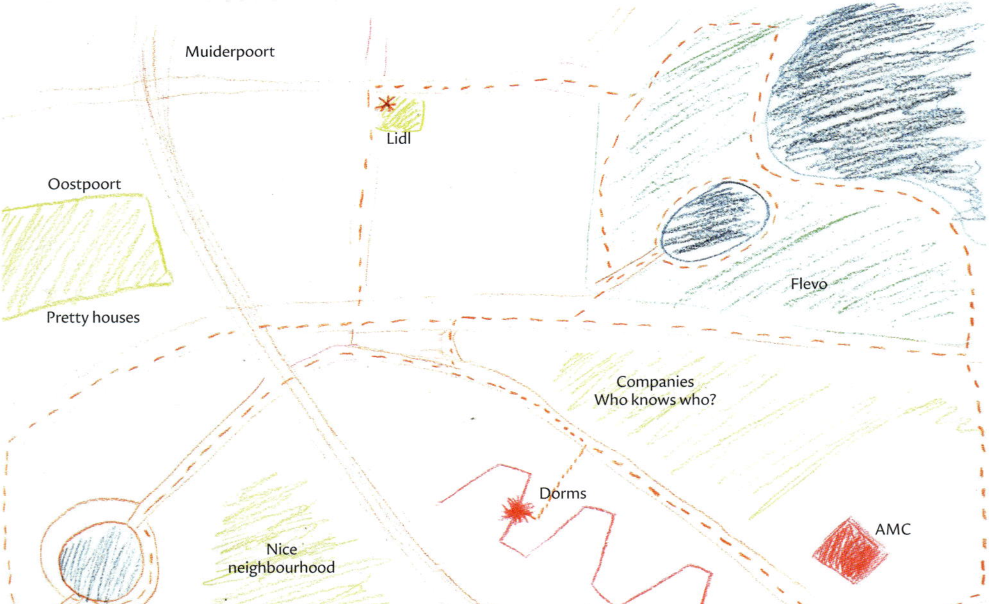

Amsterdam from the dorm
Arcam visitor

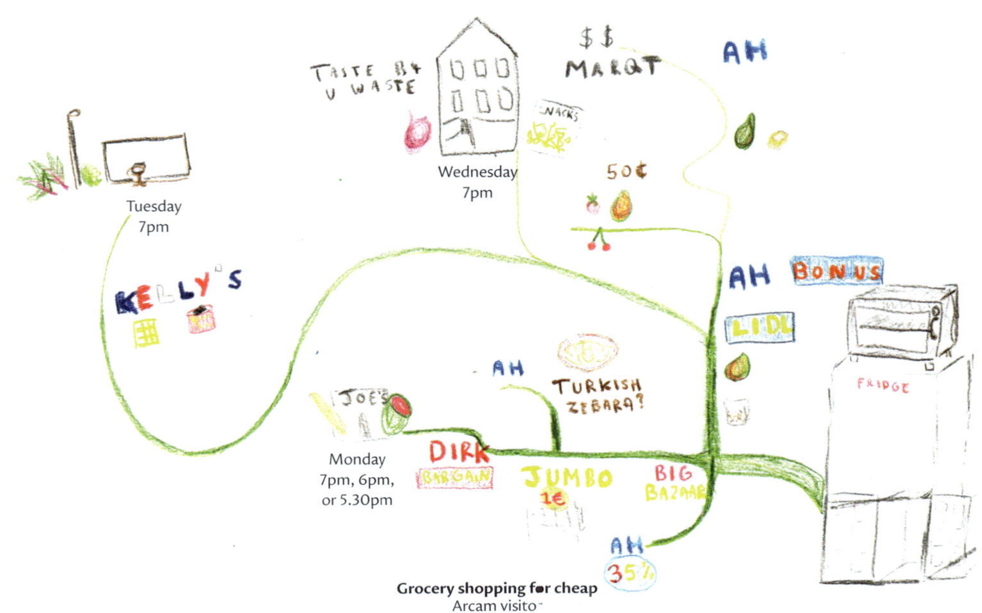

Grocery shopping for cheap
Arcam visitor

MONDAY	TUESDAY	WEDNESDAY	THURSDAY	FRIDAY	SATURDAY	SUNDAY
€58 – €15 = €43	€43 – €13 = €30	€30 – €15 = €15	€15 – €11 = €4	€4 – €2 = €2	€2 – €2 = €0	€0

Enough is not enough
Hayat: 'When you live in an asylum seeker's centre in the Netherlands, you receive €58 each week to cover all costs. This is not enough to survive.'

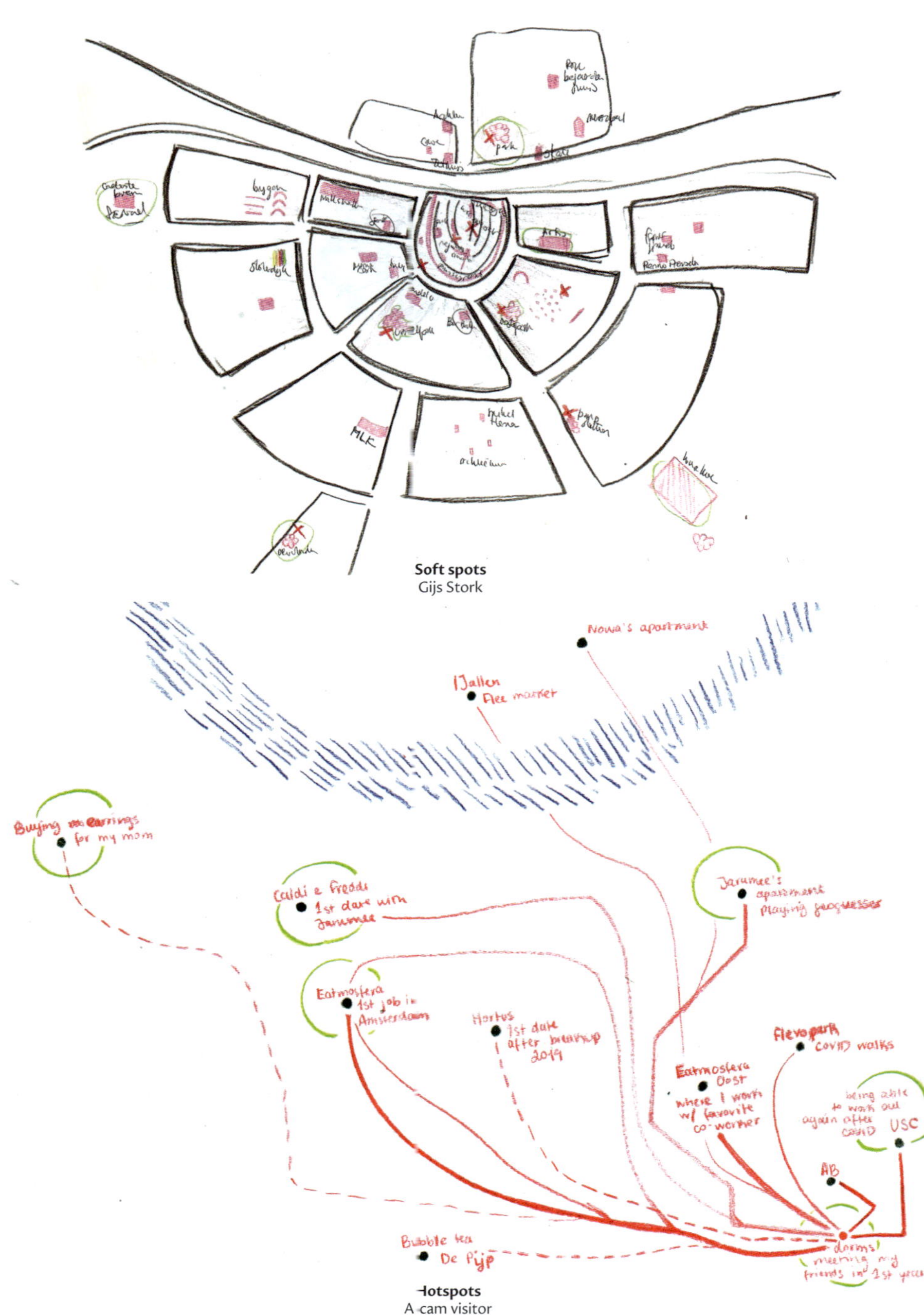

Soft spots
Gijs Stork

Hotspots
A cam visitor

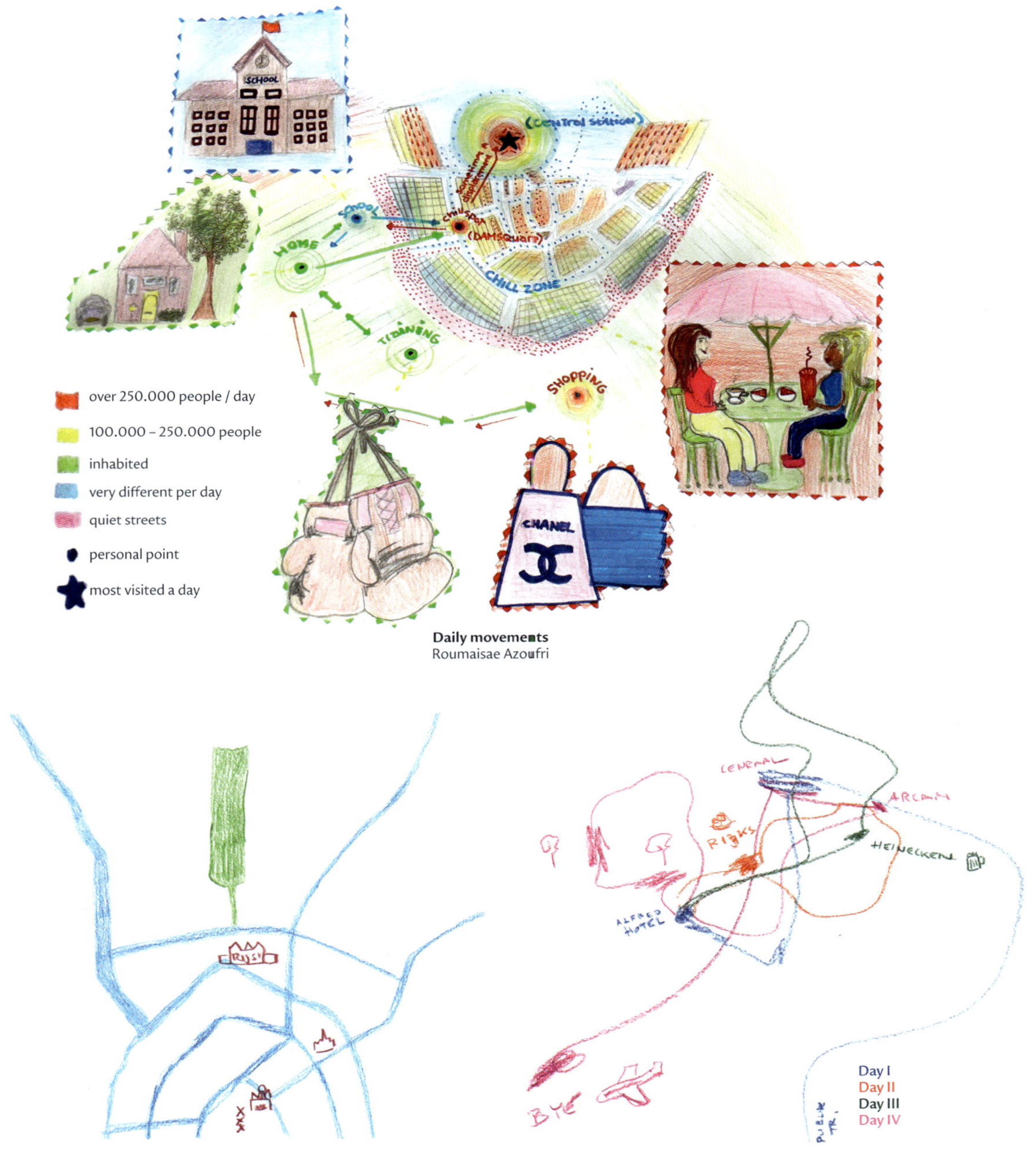

over 250.000 people / day

100.000 – 250.000 people

inhabited

very different per day

quiet streets

personal point

most visited a day

Daily movements
Roumaisae Azoufri

Veins
Arcam visitor

Four days in Amsterdam
Arcam visitor

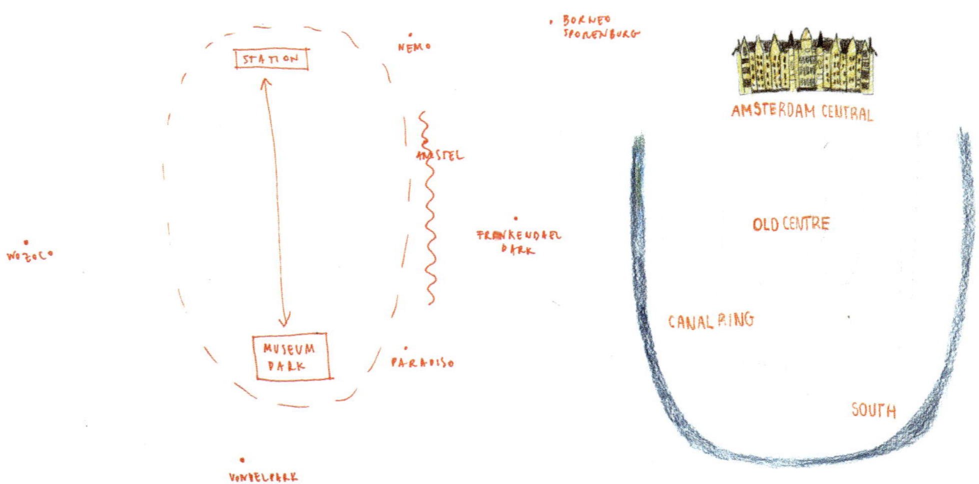

Two cities of Amsterdam

Ludo: 'The first city is where I bring my friends that come for the first time, the second city is the one I experience alone, when I follow my passions and interests: outside the dotted line.'

Central
Tara Lane

Cycling, walking
Arcam visitor

Habitual perspective
Arcam visitor

Geuzenveld, a playground surrounded by buildings
Merna Gomaa

Canta-stad
Arcam visitor: 'The Canta is a motorised vehicle in the form of a small car that can drive a maximum speed of 45 km per hour.
You don't need a driver's licence to drive the Canta. You can ride it on the bike paths and park it anywhere.
In the narrow streets of the centre of Amsterdam, the Cantas are an indispensable part of the street scene.'

Connectivity

Finn van Tol: 'On a beautiful, cloudless day, I recommend walking around Zeedijk and Nemo and spending some time looking skyward. Against the background of Amsterdam, high above the busy, diverse mix of tourists and residents, a private jet silently flies past every five minutes. The hub Schiphol offers up this small display, giving us insight into the enormous number of super-rich people in the world. As quietly as these private planes glide by in the background amidst the din of the city centre, huge passenger planes roar just as loudly over the quiet Bijlmer neighbourhood.'

Boathouse
Arcam visitor

Boathouse
Piotr

***Our tent at Zeeburg camping**
Arcam visitor

Life in the aquarium
Arcam visitor
Glass on façades

Bloemgracht, Jordaan
Arcam visitor

Coordinated by Vesla and Ramanda, and thanks to the support of youth social workers from the local organisation Swazoom, Bijlm3r organised a workshop for children from the Southeast borough. For a day, these kids traded the(ir) Anansi community centre in the D-zone for the architectural centre Arcam in the centre of the city. Most of them are from the area Venserpolder. The assignment was to create a series of

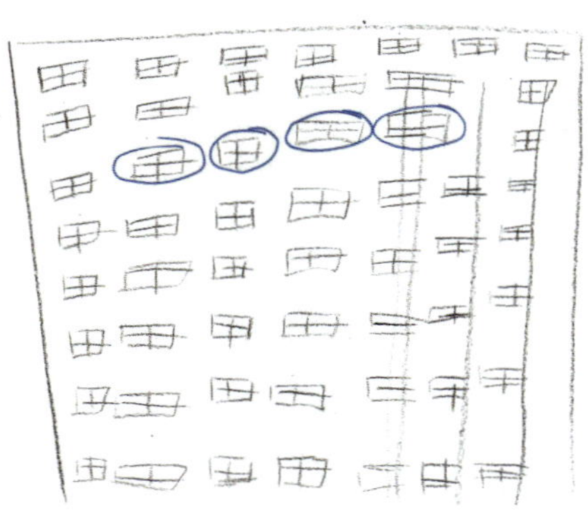

'Venserpolder'
The children who participated in the workshop are most familiar with the area of Venserpolder. They characterise the neighbourhood's identity with its closed apartment blocks, while some drew elements that signify their individuality within the blocks' uniformity.

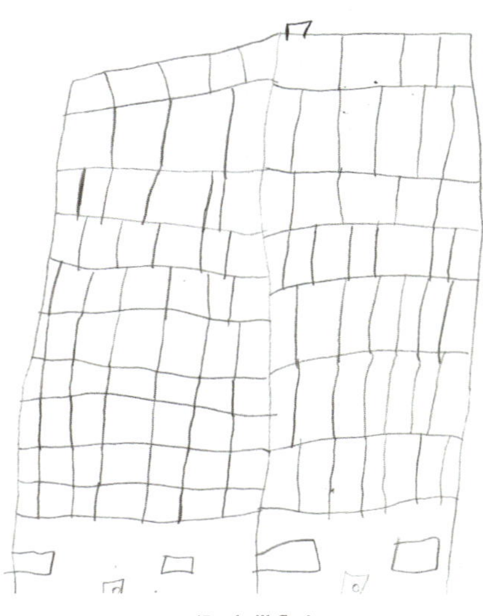

'Daalwijkflat'
Daalwijk is the only remaining original honeycomb flat in the D-buurt (D-zone) that has partly survived major demolition and transformation resulting from the 1992–2010 large-scale redevelopment.

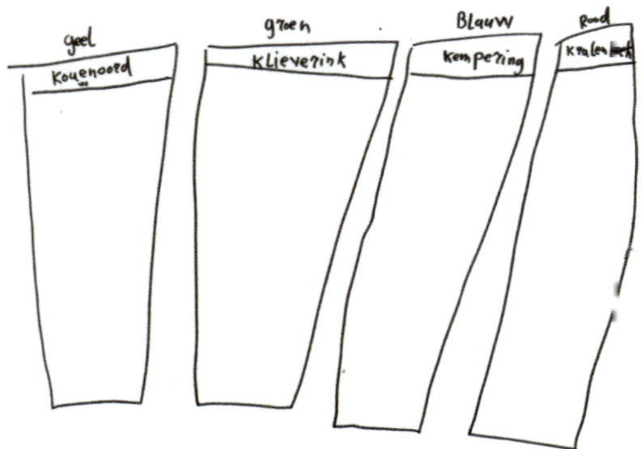

'K-buurt'
These four highrise towers stand tall in the K-buurt (K-zone) along a primary street Karspeldreef. At night, the colourful lighting provides a pallet that is visible from within and outside the borough.

'H-buurt'
A well-known part of the H-buurt is a central square with a playground and a stall selling snacks and candy. The locals call the square 'Kraampje' (refering to the little stall selling snacks) or 'Pleintje' (little square).

drawings of 'letterbuurten' since most zones in the borough are systemically named according to alphabetic order. The children first discussed the characteristics of the neighbourhoods using spider diagrams and then made drawings of their spatial characteristics.

'Rabobank'
Primarily referred to as 'Het Zandkasteel' (The Sandcastle), this monumental and iconic building complex meanders through the central shopping centre 'Amsterdamse Poort'. It is the former ING bank headquarters, originally NMB, and is now a housing complex with additional commercial provisions and facilities.

'Our Domain'
Located near the Holendrecht area of the Southeast borough, this contemporary apartment building (OurDomain East House) is featured in architectural discussions and included on Arcam's timeline, which the participants saw during the workshop.

'Kraaiennest'
The area of Kraaiennest (K-zone) is typically characterised by its striking original honeycomb flats, four highrise towers, the iconic mosque, a metro station, and a market. The original row-houses are often overlooked. After the 1992–2010 redevelopment, which also took place along the 's-Gravendijkdreef in the K-zone, more row-houses replaced highrise flats.
This drawing is a unique and unexpected testimony of these 21st century row-houses.

'Kraainest'
Various areas are experienced as shopping centres.
Particular shops and brands are factors that contribute
to collective memory, identification, and experience.

'Centrum Strandvlietpad'
Some areas are known because of their metro station,
such as Strandvliet, which is actually in Venserpolder. E-buurt (E-zone)
has a cycling road named Strandvlietpad. The systematic naming is
confusing but amenities and services tend to become local landmarks,
such as those small food stalls like 'Kraampje' in Gein and H-buurt.

'Dalsteinerdreef'
Main roads are often named 'dreef'. and the Venserpolder area is
accessible via Dalsteindreef and Dolingadreef. This drawing shows
a courtyard with a focus on the vegetation and playground equipment.

'Metro Ganzenhoef en Venserpolder'
Metro stations are gateways to areas such as Venserpolder and
Ganzenhoef. They are strong elements in the identification of neigh-
bourhoods. Alongside the track of Line 54, which passes the Strandvliet
Station, you will regularly see regional NS (yellow/blue) trains speed by.

'Venserpolder'
Note by the illustrator: 'It has a lot of car roads,
there is a lot of tires, it has a lot of colour, there is a big building,
it is big, and there are a lot of parks.'

'Bijlmer Park Theater'
The Bijlmer Parktheater (located at Anton de Komplein, a square connected
to Nelson Mandelapark, formerly known and often referred to as Bijlmerpark) offers
activities and events. The theatre is a central place for theatre and related (youth) programmes.
It is well known among most locals.

I've lived in various asylum seeker reception centres. I've had two temporary youth rental contracts. Rents are rising every month, and social housing is disappearing all around me. Making ends meet in Amsterdam feels unstable and insecure. The fact that housing has become an investment is more and more apparent each day. Investors have different priorities than mine, I know that for sure.

De Dam
Eid
Dam Square is the iconic square where hippies used to camp out in the 1970s. It's being flooded with tourists, it's being used by street performers to earn their living, it's being avoided by locals. But it's also a place to blend in with the crowd and enjoy the buzz around you.

Shadi Srewel

BOHEMISH

I miss Syria and my old city of Damascus, where the city centre is bustling and full of life. It's intense and yet slow at the same time; everything flows and moves naturally—in total inefficiency. I love the streets full of people, the food, and the music. Sometimes I go to Dam Square for its hustle and bustle and exuberance. Here it sometimes feels a bit like home, so *bohemish*, to let go of your worries, to live in the now—that feeling.

When I arrived in Amsterdam, these were the only places I knew. In the winter shelter and the World House, people who arrive in Amsterdam without documents can find shelter and help, but I liked to hang out at the public library (OBA).

At the OBA I am not seen as the refugee, unlike in the other places; I can just submerge into the crowd and read books.

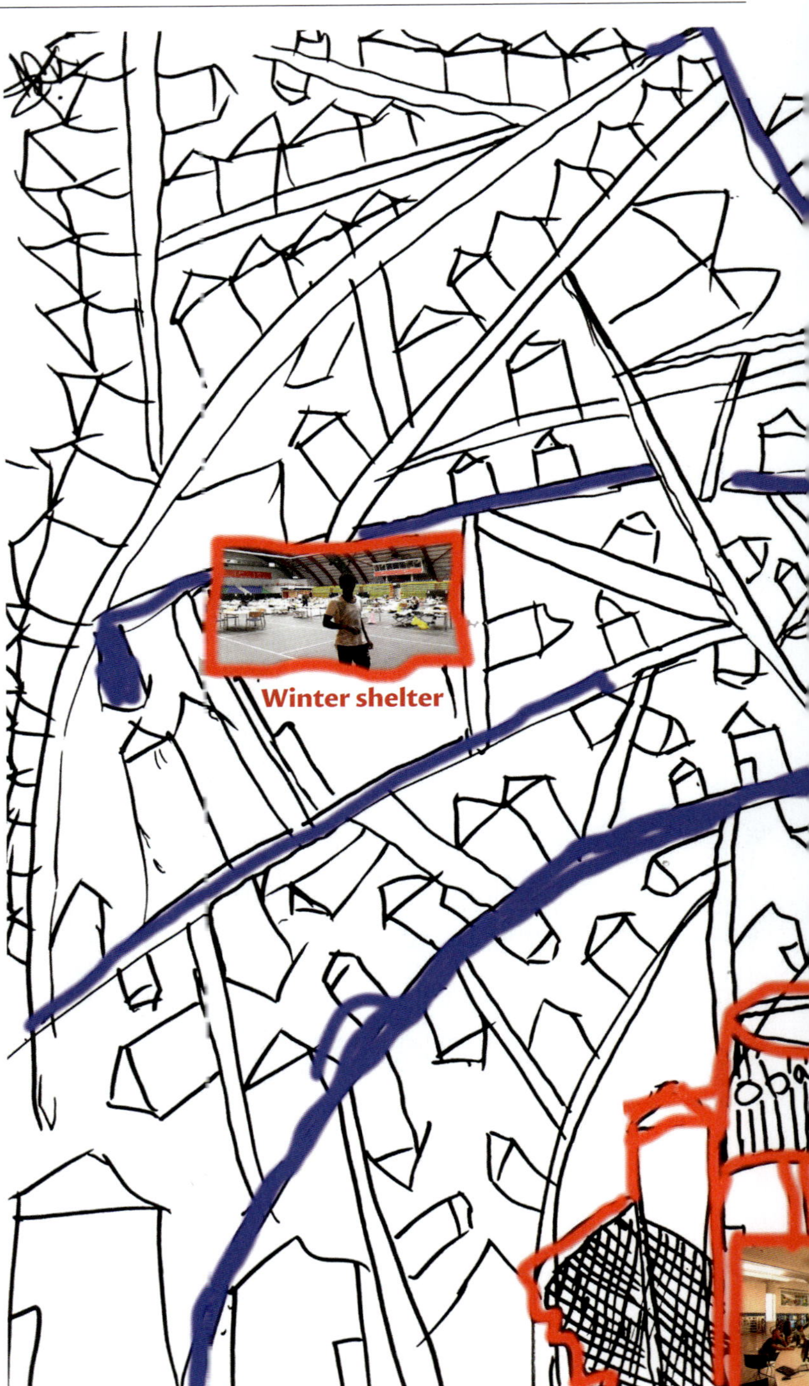

World House
OBA

1 I was transferred from Emmeloord to an AZC (Centre for Asylum Seekers) in Amsterdam. I just got a new bicycle that could not be taken on the bus. So I decided to cycle all the way to Amsterdam. 2 Broek in Waterland: simply nice. 3 Amsterdam-Oost: to get some bissap juice at my fellow countryman's place. 4 Almere: When the weather is nice and I want to exercise. 5 Durgerdam: visiting my Dutch family.

When I cycle, I always have a destination to go to and never just ride around without direction. To break this goal-oriented pattern of navigation, I decided to cycle without knowing where to go. I didn't use any maps, but instead used navigational guidelines I imposed on myself. The navigation app on my phone registered these random patterns as a result of my non-directional strolls.

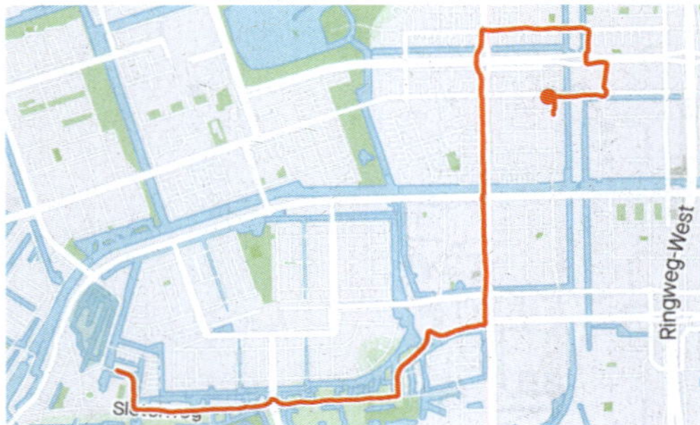

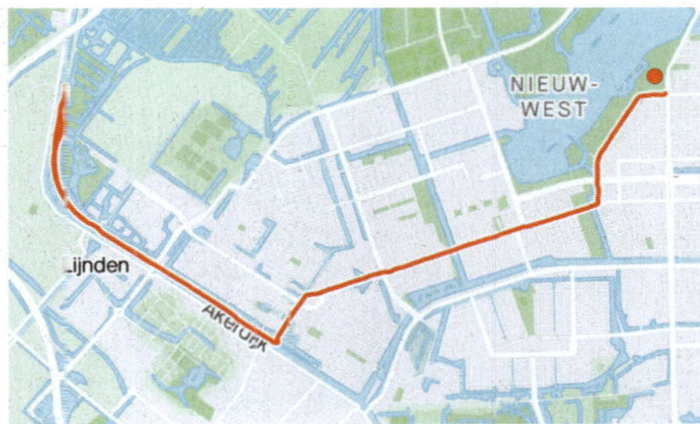

Traffic light

After stopping at a red light, I went forward, then at the second red light, I turned right, and at the third red light, I turned left. I had to change the rule as it didn't work when there weren't any traffic lights. Many times, turning right or left was not possible, because of road blocks or construction.

Sun light

Another route was following the direction of the sun throughout the route. I got cold and it was a sunny day. The result was mainly a straight path in one direction toward the west. The sun was great and I made a stop at an old windmill turned into a café somewhere along the path.

No rule

This is another path in which my route was redirected by construction works in the Hemsterhuisstraat. It looks to me like a gentrification process is taking place in this area.

Letting go

This time the rule went like this: first go right or straight forward; at the next intersection, go right again or straight forward; then at the next intersection, go left or go straight forward; and repeat it twice again; and so on. This allowed me to enjoy and experience the road. It led me to nearby areas that I would not have visited without this exercise. It was a good way to learn to let go; I trusted the rules and gave in for the experience.

HANDSHAKE WITH A STRANGER

When I move through the city on my bike, most of the time I have a clear destination. It's a journey from point A to point B that doesn't leave much space for unplanned encounters. I have noticed that many Amsterdammers lose their gloves on the busy bike lanes. Stopping at the sites of lost gloves, taking a picture, and sometimes picking them up, I found a way to integrate unplanned breaks and encounter strangers.

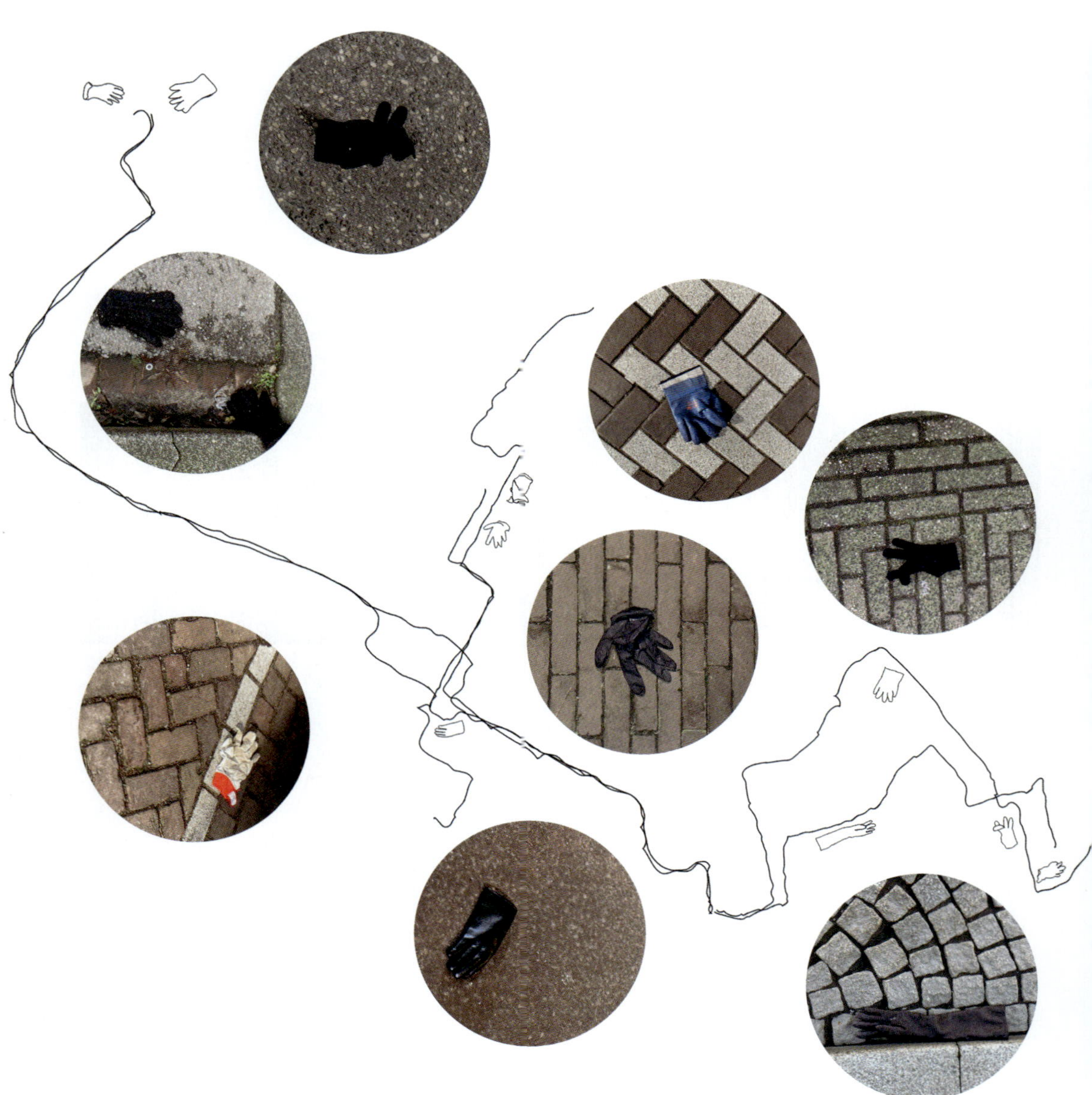

Nell Bucher

UNFORESEEABLE ADVENTURES

Cruising through Amsterdam with a motor boat is a one-of-a-kind experience. Imagine how it feels to own a boat: it can bring you wherever you wish, whenever you want. With our little ferry boat, called Tobias Spot 108, my friends and I discovered Amsterdam in a unique way, one that no bike culture can introduce you to. It brought us unforeseeable adventures across a city that constantly surprises you. This map shows an outline of the classic routes we cruised with Tobias, passing by all my favourite places.

Janfrans van der Eerden

THE GAY WEB

This map shows how I spun my web of routes across the city as a gay man over the years. These are the places I visited regularly, or where special events took place. They highlight both positive and negative experiences, divided into a number of themes.

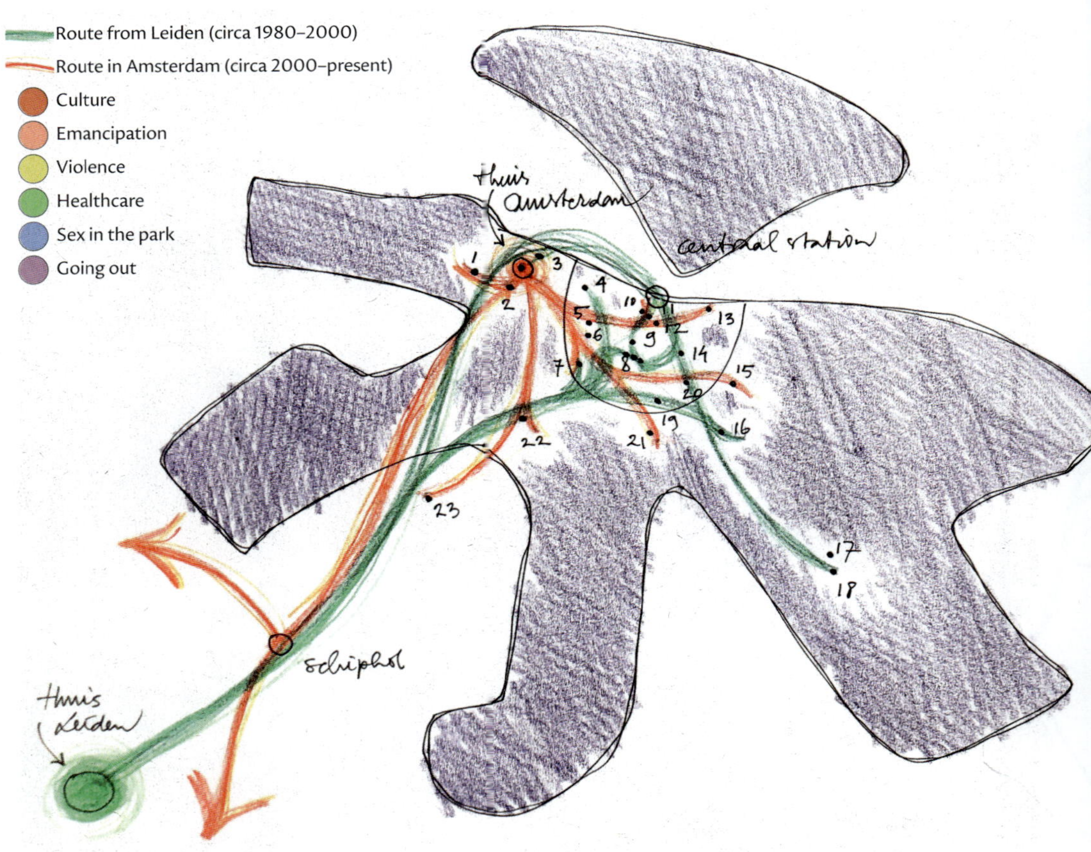

1. Oud-Roze photo exhibition

2. Roze Stadsdorp gatherings

3. Attending the Roze Filmdagen, Ketelhuis, Westerpark

4. Cafe de Vink, Vinkenstraat

5. Commemorations at the Homo-monument, Westermarkt

6. Second COC Netherlands location (LGBTQI rights org.), Rozenstraat

7. Performances in the Stads-schouwburg/ITA, Leidseplein

8. Bars and nightclubs along the Reguliersdwarsstraat

9. Browsing at Boekhandel Vrolijk, Palace Street

10. The Web, the Cuckoo's Nest, Nieuwezijds Kolk and Sint Jacobsstraat

11. My GP, Koestraat

12. The Cockring nightclub, Warmoesstraat

13. Visits and meetings at IHLIA, at the OBA (library)

14. Getting tested at the GGD venereal disease clinic

15. Oosterpark

16. Coming out at my job in the old Wibaut house

17. Robbery Fleerde, Bijlmermeer

18. Photo recognition at the Bijlmermeer police station

19. First COC Netherlands location, Frederiksplein

20. To the opera at the Stopera, Waterlooplein

21. Sarphatipark

22. Rozentuin, Vondelpark

23. De Nieuwe Meer, De Oeverlanden park

Board meeting ILGA via Schiphol and by train to Brussels

A STUDENT'S FAVOURITE QUEER CLUBS

The famous Reguliersdwarsstraat* has a lot of queer clubs. From there it's very easy to cycle to other clubs.

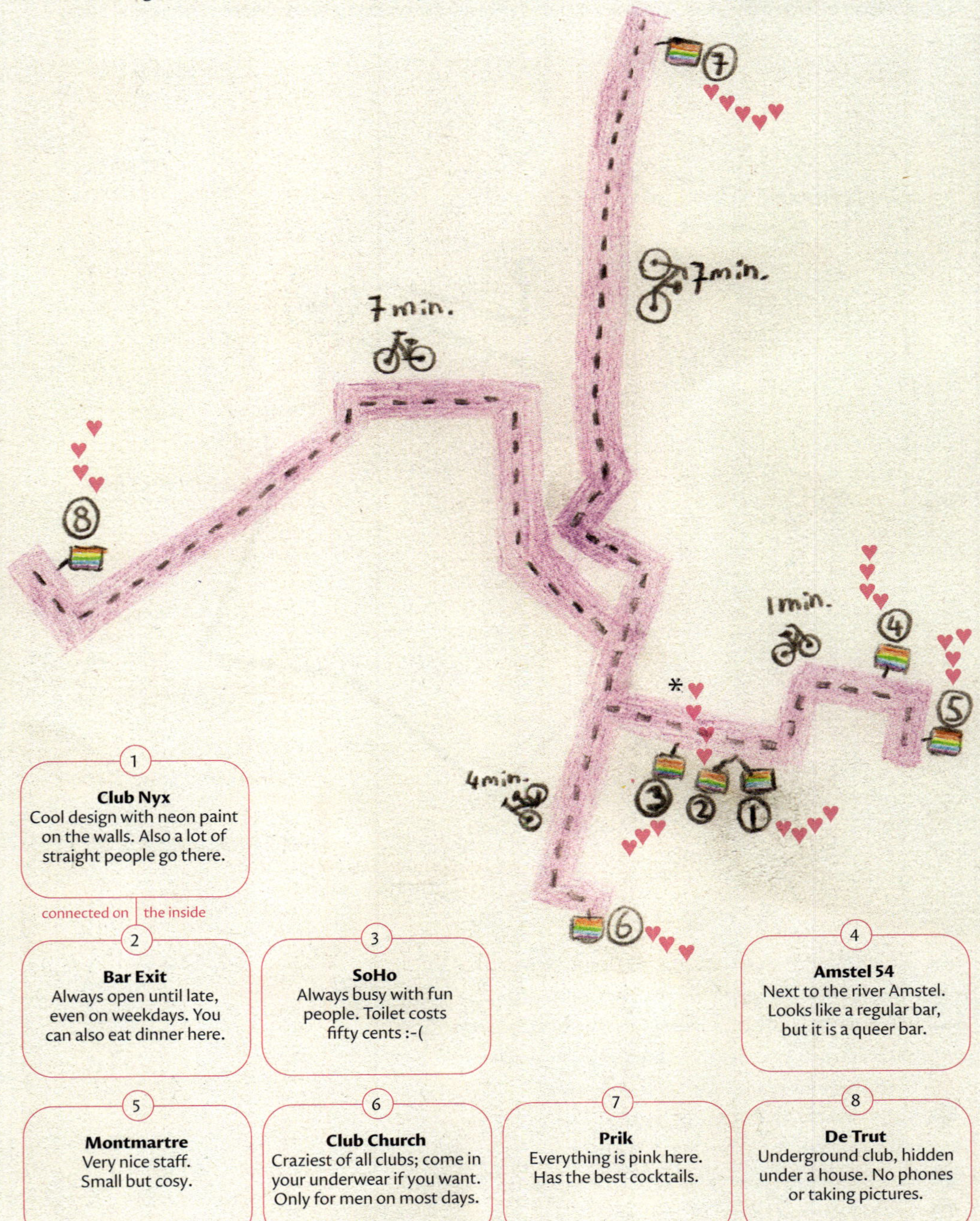

1

Club Nyx
Cool design with neon paint on the walls. Also a lot of straight people go there.

connected on | the inside

2

Bar Exit
Always open until late, even on weekdays. You can also eat dinner here.

3

SoHo
Always busy with fun people. Toilet costs fifty cents :-(

4

Amstel 54
Next to the river Amstel. Looks like a regular bar, but it is a queer bar.

5

Montmartre
Very nice staff. Small but cosy.

6

Club Church
Craziest of all clubs; come in your underwear if you want. Only for men on most days.

7

Prik
Everything is pink here. Has the best cocktails.

8

De Trut
Underground club, hidden under a house. No phones or taking pictures.

ROUTES OF PROTEST

On this map, you can see the routes of the various protest marches and demonstrations I have participated in. Though Amsterdam is often depicted as an idyll, I put Amsterdam on the map as a place of protest.

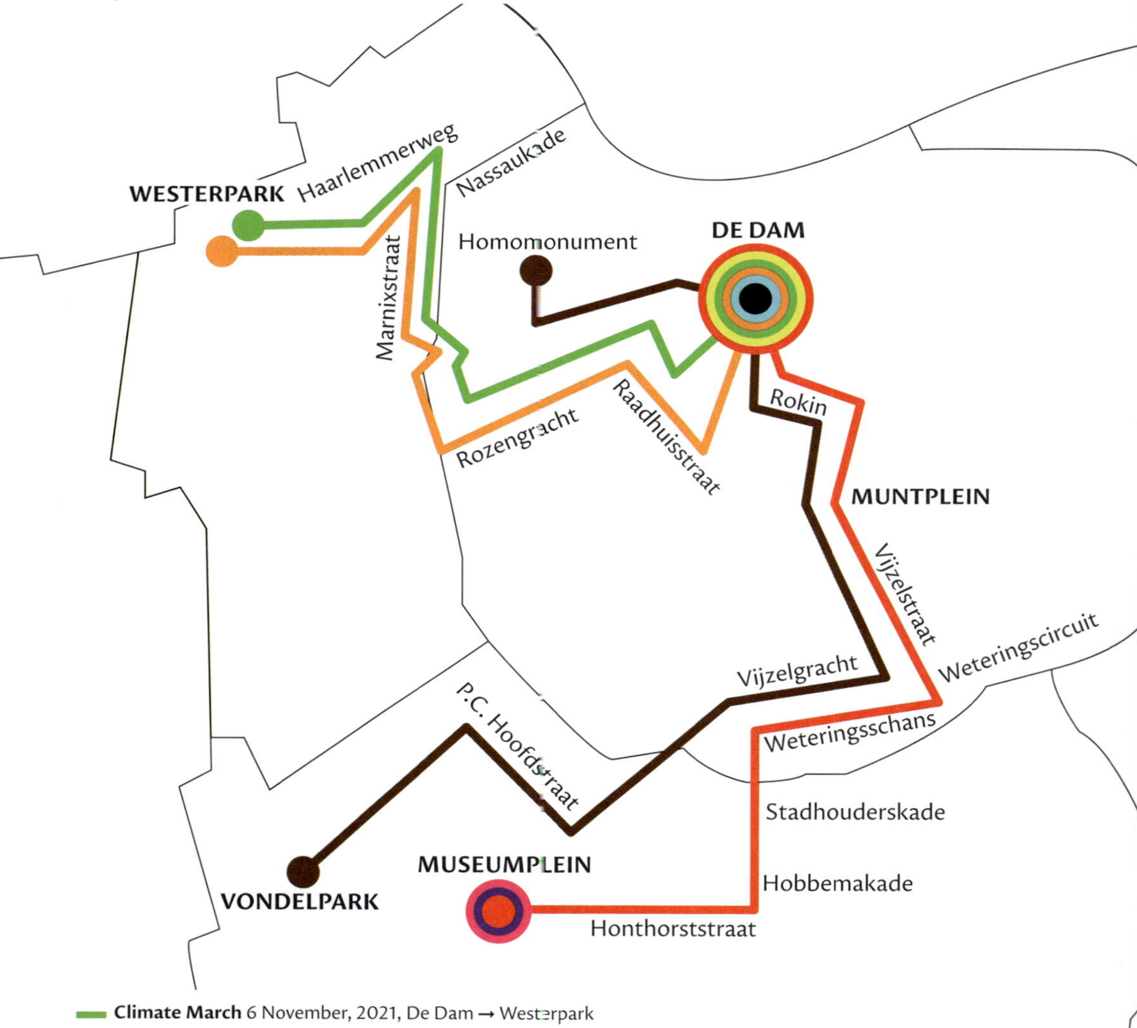

Climate March 6 November, 2021, De Dam → Westerpark

Housing Protest 12 September, 2021, Westerpark → De Dam

Pridewalk 30 July, 2021, Homomonument → Vondelpark

Womensmarch 2 October, 2021, Dam Square → Museumplein

The Voice Protest 29 January, 2022, Museumplein

Loan System Protest 5 February, 2022, Museumplein

Ukraine Protest 27 February, 2022, The Dam

Black Lives Matter Protest 1 June, 2020, Dam Square

Me Too Protest 29 January, 2022, Dam Square

As a teenager in Amsterdam, you have to find your own places to chill. This subjective map shows the best chill-out spots for under-18s.

Ravi Blits

TRASH-URES

Electronic trash can be found on the streets of Amsterdam on a daily basis. The life cycle of these electronics, which are often made up of raw materials mined in different parts of the world, ends in Amsterdam. As an urban scavenger, I found these trashures between January and February 2022 and took them home to create new things.

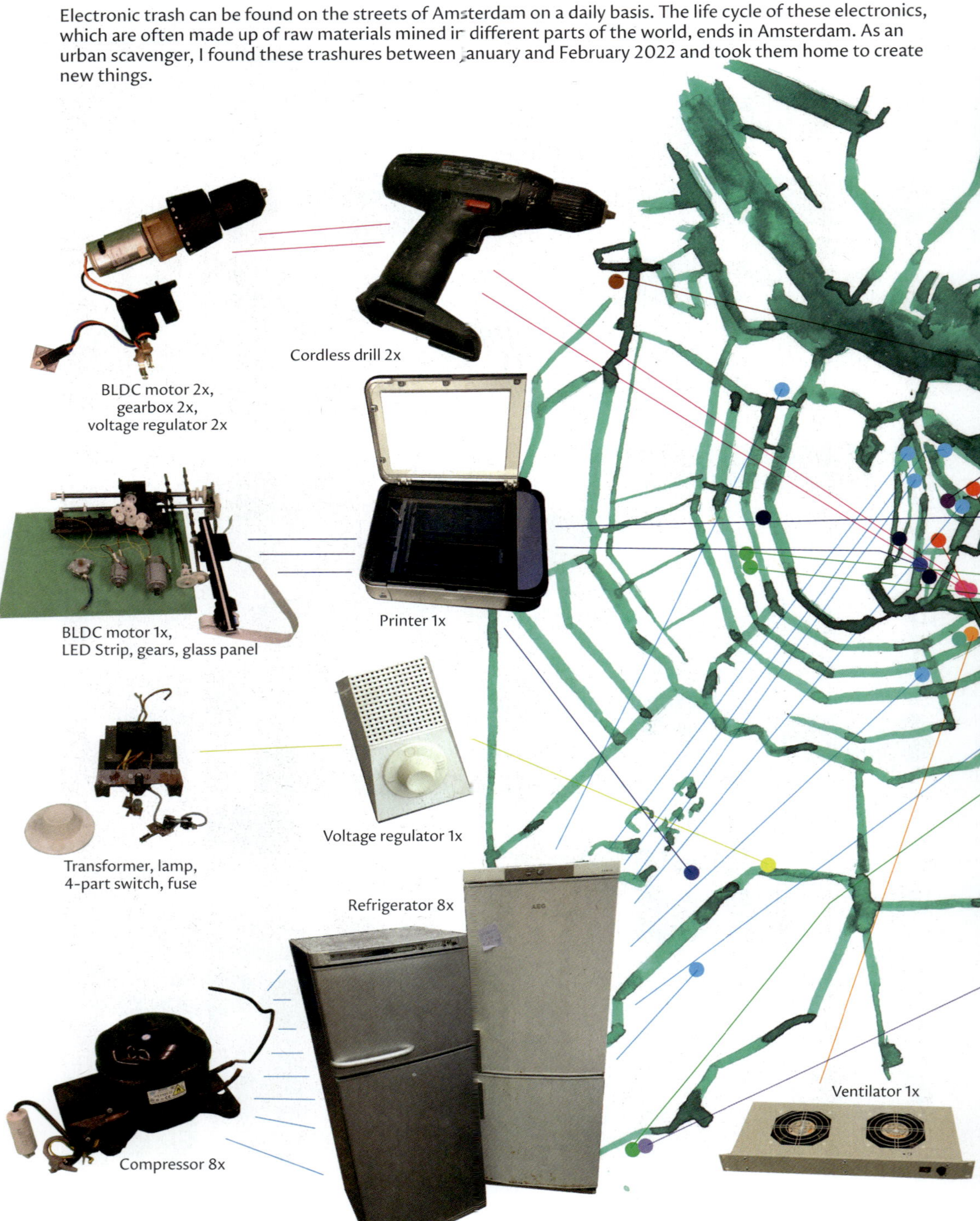

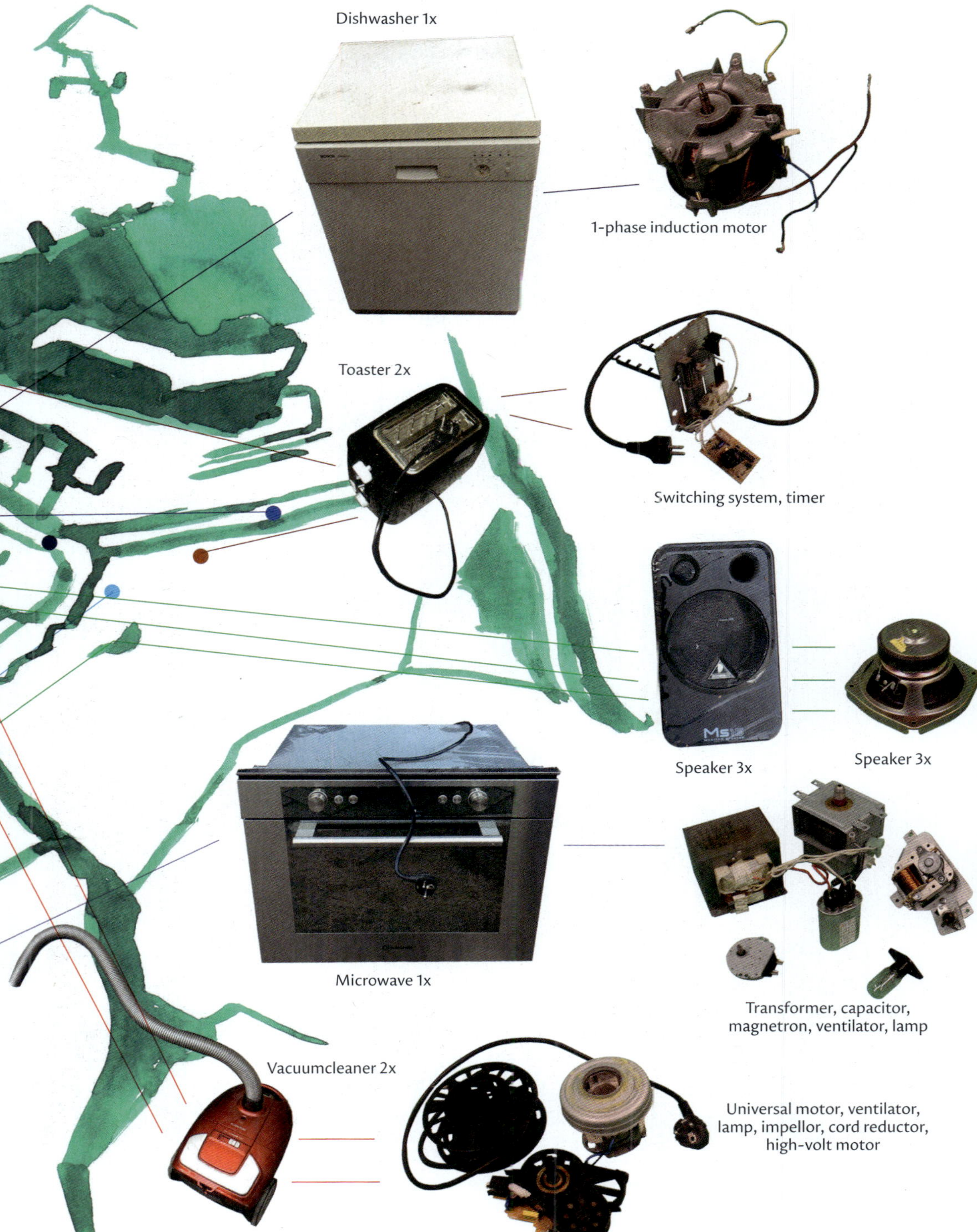

Dishwasher 1x
1-phase induction motor
Toaster 2x
Switching system, timer
Speaker 3x
Speaker 3x
Microwave 1x
Transformer, capacitor, magnetron, ventilator, lamp
Vacuumcleaner 2x
Universal motor, ventilator, lamp, impellor, cord reductor, high-volt motor

Sarah Saleh

WALKING THE CITY

| Vondelpark 1 | Vondelpark 2 | Vondelpark 3 | Vondelpark 4 | Javastraat 1 | Javastraat 2 |

Scan the soundscapes- QR codes to immerse yourself in a sonic snippet of various locations in Amsterdam.

These shapes come from the Arabic spelling of the transliteration (not the translation) of the title: *Subjective Atlas of Amsterdam*. The map contains the names of spaces relevant to me, with English or Dutch names, spelled in Arabic script.

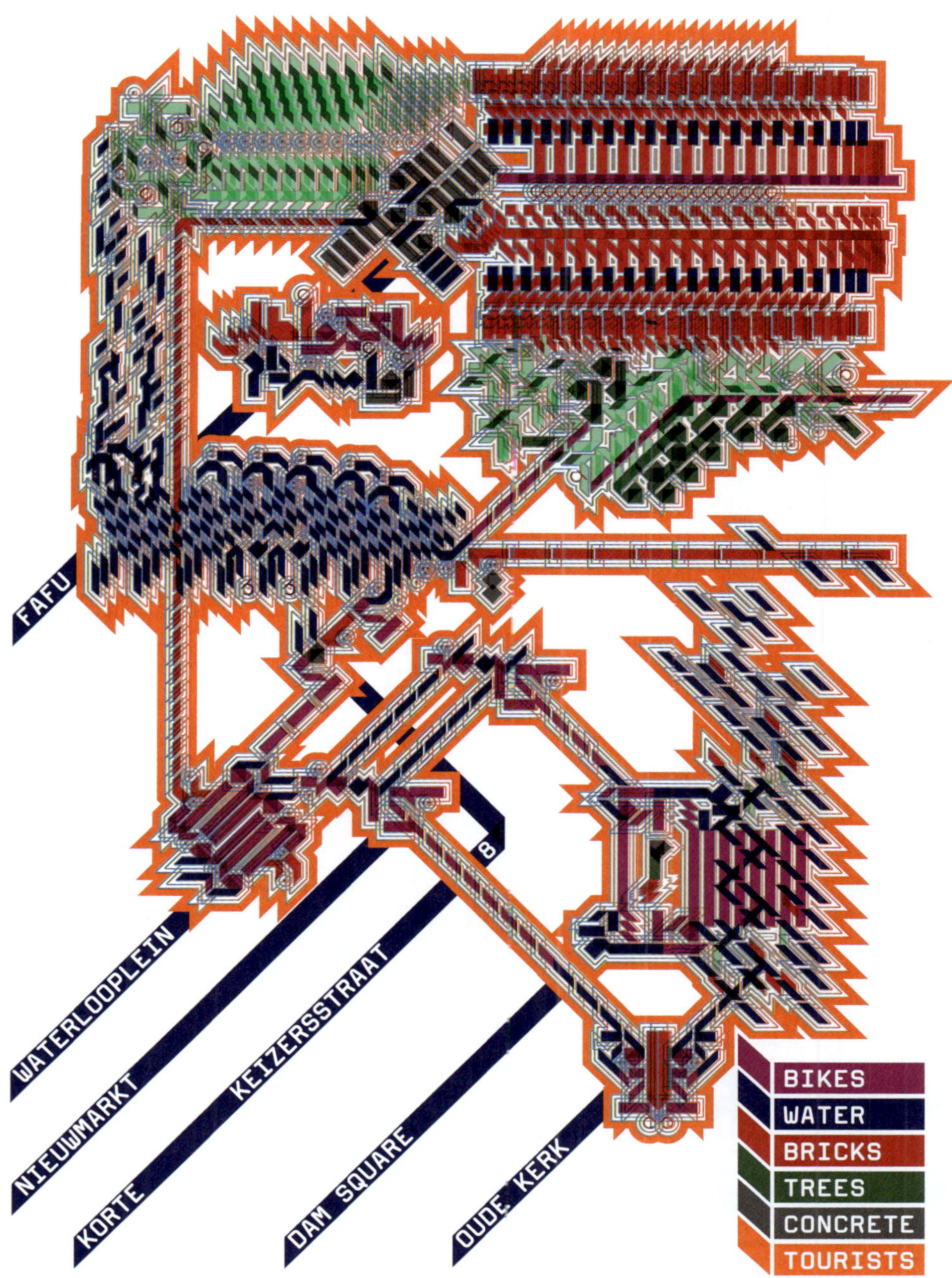

De Wallen onder controle

The Red Light District (*Wallen* in Dutch) is a unique part of Amsterdam. No other neighbourhood is so diverse, layered, and lived. Over the last few years, however, the neighbourhood has been given the image of being 'out of control' and in need of large-scale intervention. While this discourse rarely accords with reality, it became the policy ambition to transform the 'urban jungle' into a 'monumental garden'. As part of this process, more and more far-reaching measures are being introduced to increase control over the neighbourhood. While some of these measures might be framed as important for the safety of, for example, sex workers, or for a basic form of livability for inhabitants, the larger package of measures seems to be mostly directed at structurally sanitising the neighbourhood. With this map, Failed Architecture seeks to provide some insight into the complex array of measures in force as of late 2021, and kickstart a debate about their impact.

Law enforcement
Apart from police and *handhaving* (low-ranked 'law enforcers'), also 'hosts', private security guards, and traffic controllers are being deployed in the Wallen.

Closing public space
Over the years, many small streets and alleys have been closed to the public. A few close in the evening at 6pm, only to open again the following morning.
» PERMANENTLY CLOSED ALLEY
» TEMPORARILY CLOSED ALLEY

Crowd control
The corona law created the possibility of introducing a crowd-control system to the Wallen, enforcing one-way pedestrian movement at certain times.
» ONE-WAY PEDESTRIAN FLOW
» CHECKPOINT

Camera surveillance
Remote-controlled police surveillance cameras have been installed throughout the area, the locations of which have never been made public.
» POLICE CAMERA
» PUBLIC SPACE COVERED BY CAMERA SURVEILLANCE
» PUBLIC SPACE NOT COVERED BY CAMERA SURVEILLANCE

Sensors
Throughout the Wallen, counting sensors measure the number of people in the area using various techniques, some of which include video recordings.
» COUNTING SENSOR

Closing down sex workers' windows
Over the last few years, the number of windows available to sex workers has drastically diminished as a result of myriad financial and legal procedures.
22   22 » NUMBER OF CLOSED SEX WORKERS' WINDOWS PER BLOCK

Limitations on sex work in the general bylaw
In Amsterdam's general bylaw there are various stipulations with regard to 'window prostitution', which have resulted in all kinds of limitations for sex workers.

Nuisance area and removal orders
The Wallen is part of the officially indicated 'nuisance area', renewed on 1 July, 2021 for the entire city centre, which, among other things, outlaws being together as a group.

Guided tour ban
From spring 2020, the municipality has made regulations regarding guided tours stricter, including a complete ban on guided tours for a large part of the Wallen.
» BOUNDARY OF THE GUIDED TOUR BAN AREA

Alcohol ban
A complete ban on the consumption of alcohol is in force in the entire public space of the Wallen (as well as a few surrounding streets and urban areas), punishable with a €95 fine.
++++ » BOUNDARY OF THE ALCOHOL BAN AREA

Alcohol sale ban
The Amsterdam municipality's corona measures included a temporary ban on the sale of alcohol which exclusively covered the Wallen area.
» BOUNDARY OF THE ALCOHOL
SALE BAN AREA

Street music ban
The Wallen are almost completely covered by new regulations banning street artists from performing in public space, with Nieuwmarkt and Dam being notable exceptions.
» BOUNDARY OF THE STREET MUSIC BAN AREA

Airbnb ban
Since 2021 onwards there are obligations in force to obtain a permit, register and notify any short term rentals

Behavioural instructions
Across the neighbourhood, signs have been put up to influence the behaviour of visitors, and to inform them about the various rules and regulations, such as the local alcohol ban.
» SIGN WITH BEHAVIOURAL INSTRUCTIONS

Protests and events
Local conditions are always taken into account in the procedure regulating protests and provision of event permits, which in practice limit the possibilites on the Wallen.

Optional: coffeeshops for residents only
The so-called i-criterion stipulates that only people residing in the Netherlands are allowed to access coffeeshops, which, if enforced, will have a major impact on the Wallen.

Optional: fence
In recent times multiple references have been made to completely fencing of the Wallen, with similar discussions going on about potential access gates, access passes and entry fees.

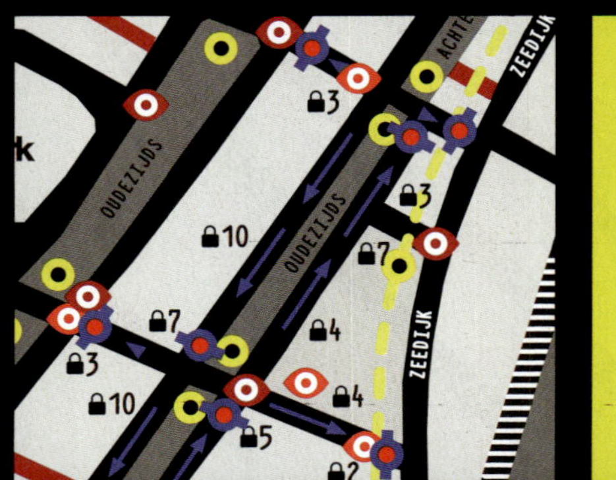

N
PRINS HENDRIKKADE
Damrak
DAMRAK
Beurs van Berlage
BEURSPLEIN
ARMSTEEG
HEINTJE HOEKSSTEEG
LANGE NIEZEL
VOORBURGWAL
ZEEDIJK
ACHTERBURGWAL
GELDERSEKADE
Oude Kerk
WARMOESSTRAAT
ST ANNENSTR.
OUDEZIJDS
OUDEZIJDS VOORBURGWAL
OUDEZIJDS ACHTERBURGWAL
WARMOESSTRAAT
ST JANSSTRAAT
Dam
NATIONAAL MONUMENT
Nieuwmarkt
ROKIN
NES
DAMSTRAAT
OUDE DOELENSTR.
OUDE HOOGSTRAAT
ACHTERGRACHT
ST. ANTONIEBREESTRAAT
KLOVENIERSBURGWAL

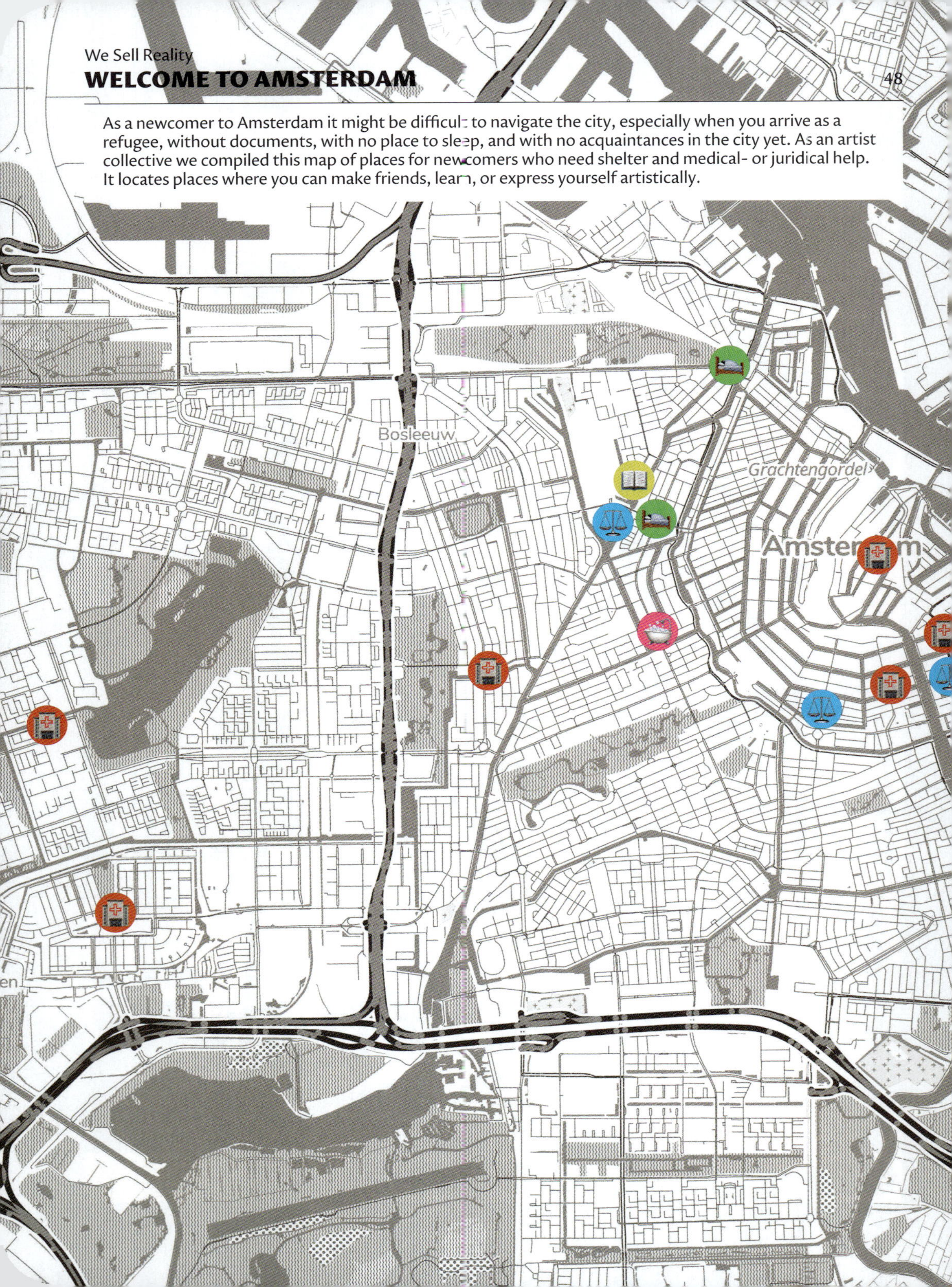

WELCOME TO AMSTERDAM

As a newcomer to Amsterdam it might be difficult to navigate the city, especially when you arrive as a refugee, without documents, with no place to sleep, and with no acquaintances in the city yet. As an artist collective we compiled this map of places for newcomers who need shelter and medical- or juridical help. It locates places where you can make friends, learn, or express yourself artistically.

't Nopeind
Zunderdorp
Ransdorp
Durgerdam
Polder IJdoorn
beckelingsc
Diemen
Duivendrecht
Diem

MEDICAL HELP

Medicijnman Apotheken Amsterdam
Utrechtsestraat 86
020-6244333

Benu Apotheek Wester
Postjesweg 101-H
020-6183114

Dokters van de Wereld
Nieuwe Herengracht 20
020-7653800

Pharmacie LeVillage BV
Osdorpplein 403
020-6190697

Sumatra Apotheek BV
Sumatrastraat 92
020-6650905

Regio Apotheek Amsterdam Ganzenhoef
Bijlmerdreef 1169
020-6954401

Apotheek Nieuw Sloten
Kempenlaan 104
020-6152075

Red Cross
Valkenburgerstraat 24
020-6226211

Kruispost
Oudezijds Voorburgwal 129
020-6249031

Equator Foundation
Nienoord 5
020-8407676

SHELTER

Vreemdelingenloket
Houtmankade 334

ASKV Steunpunt Vluchtelingen
Frederik Hendrikstraat 111-c
020-6272408

Kraakspreekuur @ Joe's Garage
Pretoriusstraat 43

HYGIENE

Badhuis da Costa en Sauna
Da Costakade 200
020-6125946

SCHOOLING

BOOST
Danie Theronstraat 2

ASKV Steunpunt Vluchtelingen
Frederik Hendrikstraat 111-c
020-6272408

Wereldhuis
Nieuwe Herengracht 18

CULTURE

We Sell Reality
wesellreality@gmail.com

PrintRights
Pieter Nieuwlandstraat 93

Framer Framed
Oranje Vrijstaatkade 71
020-7630973

JURIDICAL HELP

ASKV Steunpunt Vluchtelingen
Frederik Hendrikstraat 111-c
020-6272408
Wereldhuis
Nieuwe Herengracht 18

Vluchtelingenwerk Nederland
Surinameplein 122

Juridisch Loket
Vijzelgracht 21–25
0900-8020

Inequality within a city can manifest itself in the presence or absence of facilities depending on where you live geographically. If you look at the concentration of shared cars, shared scooters, and food delivery drivers within their respective apps, you'll notice you can hardly use these 'sharing economies' in farther-away places like Amsterdam Noord. These companies follow current dynamics, but they contribute to 'mobility poverty' in Noord at the same time.

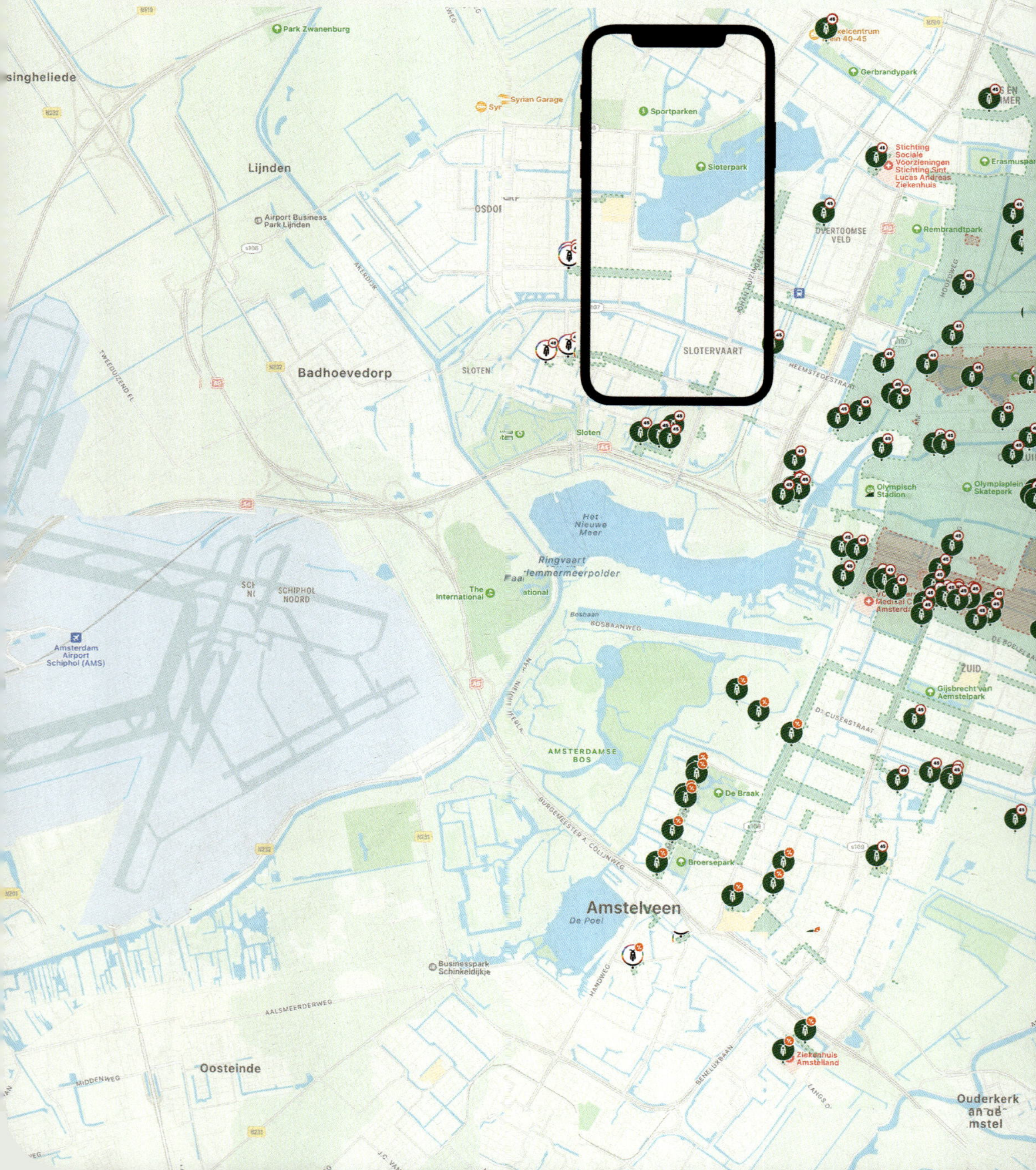

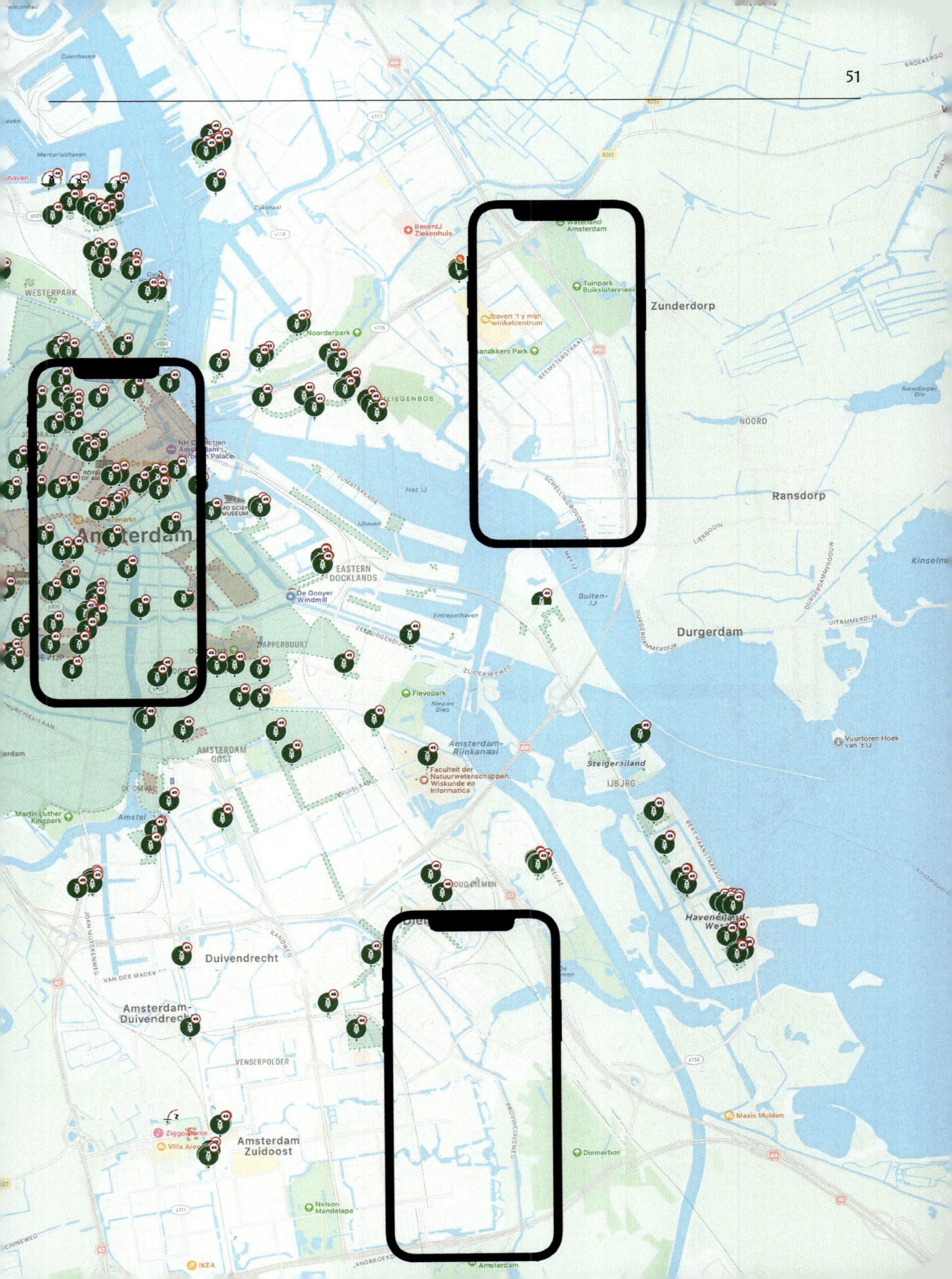
Coenhaven
Mercuriushaven
Zijkanaal
BovenIJ Ziekenhuis
Waterland Amsterdam
Tuinpark Buikslotermeer
Zunderdorp
boven 't y mijn winkelcentrum
BEEMSTERSTRAAT
WESTERPARK
Noorderpark
VLIEGENBOS
NOORD
Ransdorp
NH Collection Amsterdam
Amsterdam
SUMATRAKADE
Het IJ
IJhaven
EASTERN DOCKLANDS
De Gooyer Windmill
Buiten-IJ
Durgerdam
DURGERDAMMERDIJK
UITDAMMERDIJK
Kinselm
Entrepothaven
ZEEBURGERDIJK
DAPPERBUURT
ZUIDERZEEWEG
Flevopark
Nieuwe Diep
Amsterdam-Rijnkanaal
Faculteit der Natuurwetenschappen, Wiskunde en Informatica
Steigereiland
IJBURG
Vuurtoren Hoek van 't IJ
AMSTERDAM OOST
Martin Luther Kingpark
Amstel
DE OMVAL
OUD DIEMEN
Haveneiland-West
BEETHAANSTRAKADE
Duivendrecht
Amsterdam-Duivendrecht
VAN DER MADEWEG
JOAN MUYSKENWEG
VENSERPOLDER
PROVINCIALEWEG
Maxis Muiden
Diemerbos
Ziggo Dome
Villa Arena
Amsterdam Zuidoost
Nelson Mandelapark
IKEA
Amsterdam

I am residing at the 24-hour shelter for undocumented refugees, overlooking the Eye Museum. To me, this building is like a UFO landed in the city of Amsterdam. I connect to it as I often feel very alienated. I am here, but have no chance to really land in the city of Amsterdam.

The tour guides all say Amsterdam's city centre is the place to be. However, the people of Amsterdam know where it's actually going down: just outside of the ring road.

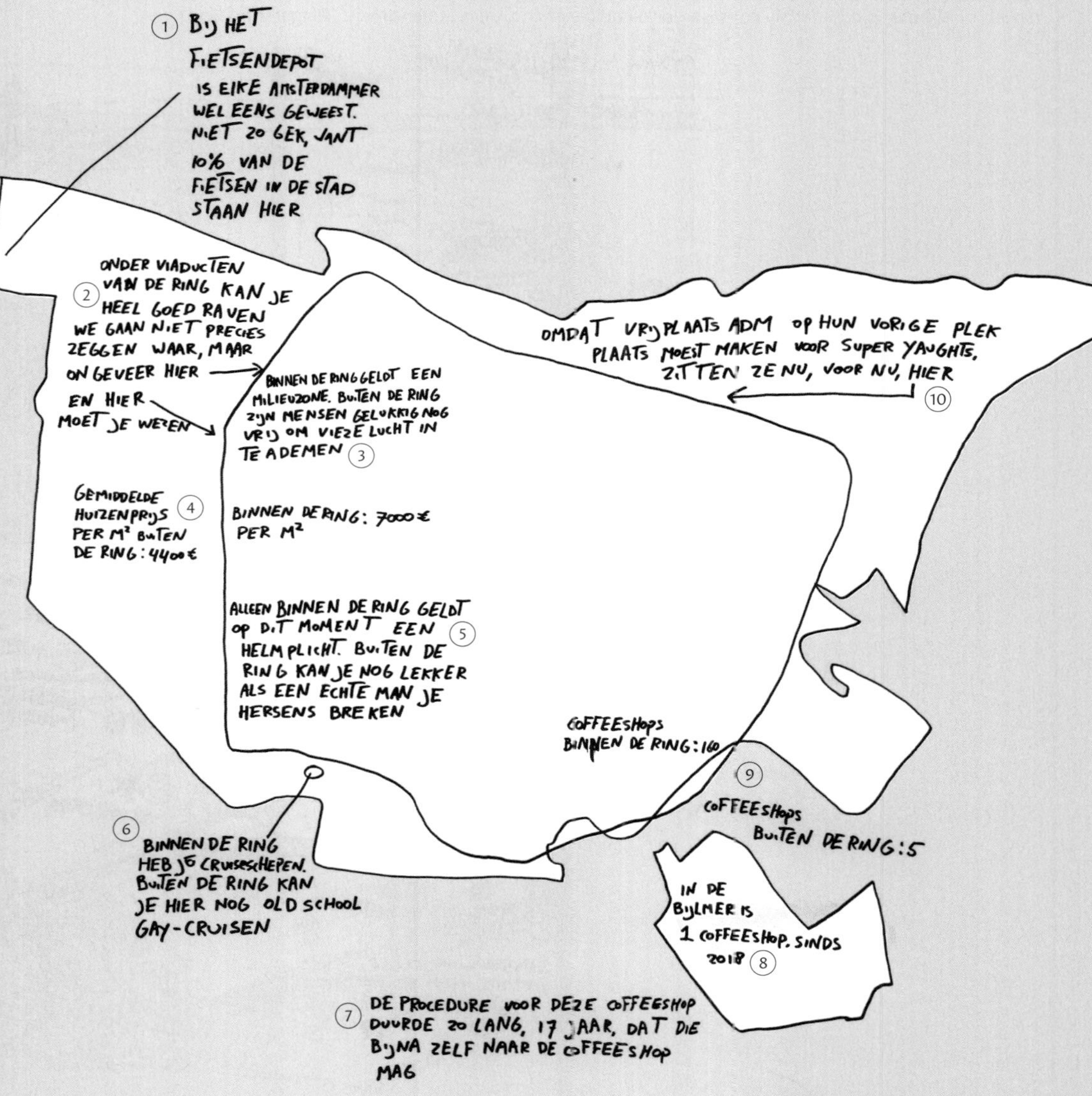

1. Every Amsterdammer has visited the city's bicycle depot at least once. Which makes sense, because 10% of all the bicycles are stranded there.
2. It's under the ring's overpasses where all the good raves are. We won't tell you exactly where, but it's close to here. And here.
3. Everything within the ring is a green zone. Luckily, outside of the ring, people still have the freedom to breathe in the pollution.
4. Average housing price outside the ring: €4,400 p/m². Within the ring: €7,000 p/m².
5. At the moment, helmets are only mandatory within the ring. Outside the ring, you're still allowed to crack your skull like a real man.
6. There are cruise ships within the ring. Outside the ring, you can still do old-school gay-cruising.
7. The application for this coffeeshop took so long, seventeen years, that it's almost old enough to be a customer there itself.
8. Since 2018, there's one coffeeshop in the Bijlmer.
9. Coffeeshops outside of the ring: 5. Coffeeshops within the ring: 160.
10. Because the ADM sanctuary, a squatters' community, had to make space for superyachts, they've been moved out here for now.

Bijlm3r collaborated with four participants, who all grew up in various areas within the neighbourhood of Gaasperdam, on mapping identities. This Map & Talk-method consists of drawing nodes, landmarks, zones, borders, icons, networks, and experiences on a base map while conducting interviews. Gaasperdam, once planned as the South of Bijlmer, is commonly considered to consist of the areas Holendrecht, Reigersbos, and Gein.

The question if Nellestein/Gaasperplas is also part of this brings about some uncertainty. From many perspectives and experiences lack detail with regard to this area. The lack of detail is also noticeable in two particular fragments of Holendrecht and Gein. These are the areas without social housing.

Holendrecht metro station (1106), as viewed from OurDomain (1105)

Kraaiennest station (1104), from Kruitberg (1104)

Kraaiennest station (1104), frcm Klieverink (1104)

(Bijlmer Museum) Station (1104), from Kruitberg (1104)

Ganzenhoef station (T103), from Geldershoofd (1103)

Ganzenhoef station (T103), from Groeneveen (1103)

Bullewijk station (1102), from Prospect Eleven (1101)

Bullewijk station (1102), from Hakfort (1102)

Hart voor de K-buurt is an organisation committed to this neighbourhood in various ways, such as the programmes we regularly organise there. We have made this map to show local residents where they can go for more information and collaboration, including meaningful places for local residents and even public toilet facilities.

Leger des Heils (Salvation Army)

Kempgarden community vegetable garden

Vliegramp (plane crash) Monument 1992

Open Atelier *Kruitberg 1002a*

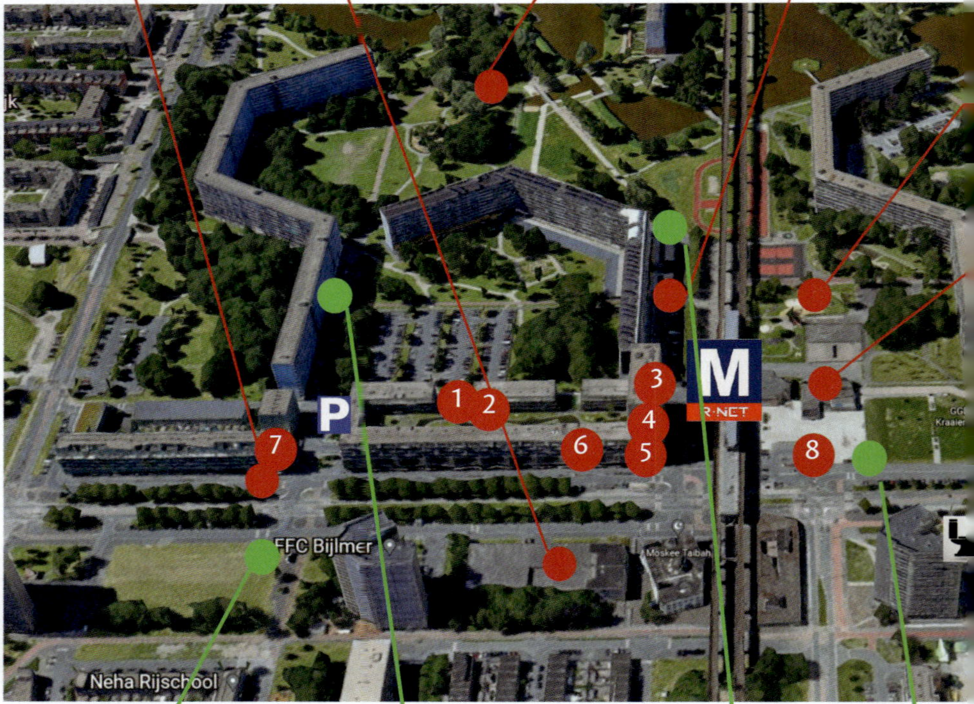

Workshop Locations

A. Across from the Leger Des Heils, on Kralenbeek field

B. At the salon, Kikkenstein flats (Nummer 2015, through the inner passage on the first floor)

C. Outside the residents' area, Kruitberg flats

D. At Klieve Hart voor de K-buurt

ground
grandmother of
iennest

Bonte Kraai
community centre

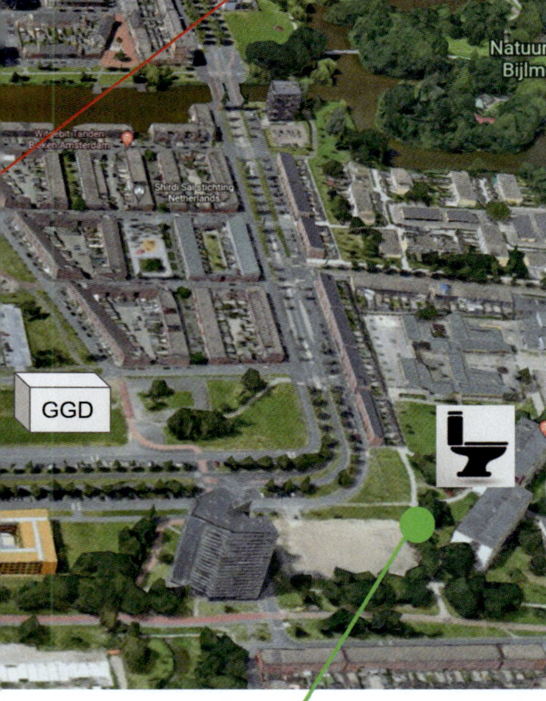

E. Next to the Koornhorst
retirement home,
on Kouwenoord field

1 Teujib Halal,
in the mall passage

2 Atouli, in the passage

3 Anytime Snack bar

4 Doner Baba

5 Fish & Chicken Corner

6 Albert Heijn grocery store

7 Leger des Heils

8 Yvette's Food Truck,
on the square

Playgrounds are where children, young people, and the elderly from Amsterdam Zuidoost come together. Not only are childhood memories created here; it is also the place where community development and social movements originate. Bartendaz, for example, organises sports matches in these parks.

Mijehof, Holendrecht

Holendrecht, Baradice

Hobbel Bobbel, Gein

Amstel III (Bijlmer West, 1105), Holendrecht, Baradice

Baradice Holendrecht, Meibergpad/Cruijff Court (a football field) in Holendrecht, Amsterdam Zuidoost

'Adidaspleintje' Holendrecht, Reigersbospad/Gaasperdam, Amsterdam Zuidoost

Voetbalveld (football field) K-buurt, Kraaiennestpad in Kraaiennest, Amsterdam Zuidoost

'Kraampje/pleintje' H-buurt, Bullewijkpad/Abcouderpad in H-buurt, Amsterdam Zuidoost

Elzenhagen Zuid is a place in full transition. A total of 2,577 trees will be felled for temporary housing, a school, and a sports hall. Eventually, the municipality expects to replant 1,100 trees and 250 shrubs in the area. With these images, I investigate alternative perspectives on the current dominating street scene.

Foreground: Plants in a radius of fifty metres around Block 6, Startblok Elzenhagen, 12 July, 2022

Background: Construction work around Startblok Elzenhagen, July 10, 2022

How should cities deal with existing and found realities? Deciding who must leave and who may stay is not an easy task, but the law must give every form of existence a chance to persist, since the right to be present is the fundamental basis upon which societies are built.

Marantha community transformation centre (Bullewijkpad 51, 1102 LB Amsterdam)
In 2018, the lawn of this well-established community centre was turned into a small public football pitch and a garden, which is not only used by the members of the religious community, but also by other neighbouring residents. As soon as development plans are decided here the garden will have to make way for new urban construction, which is why it has never received a permanent water connection.

Bij Gein Lunchroom (Hullenbergweg 1, 1101 BW Amsterdam)
By selling lunch and coffee, breeding bees, and planting a flower meadow and a small vegetable garden, the owner of Bij Gein strives to bring the neighbourhood together, providing regional foods and offering both the residents and workers in the vicinity a closer connection with nature. Although he was offered a new plot of land due to the clearance of the neighbouring building, he has been struggling with uncertain details of deadlines and construction site processes.

Tuinpark Nieuw Vredelust (Buitensingel 4, 1114 BE Amsterdam-Duivendrecht)
If it is up to the municipalities of Amsterdam and Ouder-Amstel, the garden park Nieuw Vredelust in Duivendrecht will soon have to make place for 4,500 new apartments and an expansion of the famous local football club Ajax. The site lies directly under the airport's approach line, which makes it the subject of controversial discussions between the airport operator, the garden community, and the municipalities.

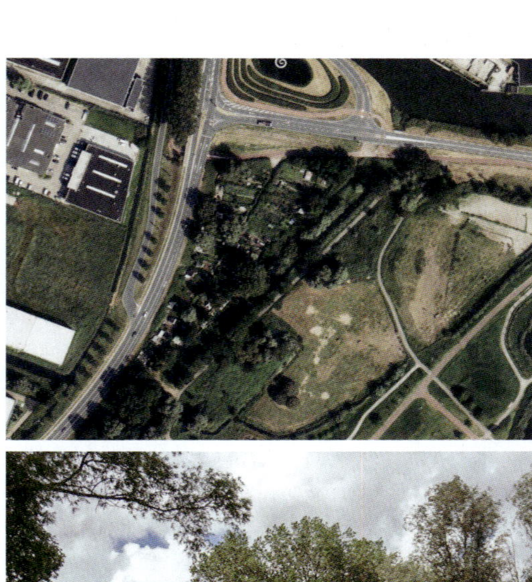

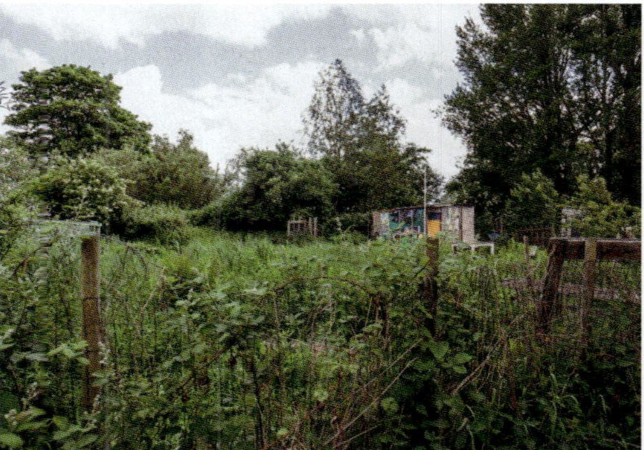

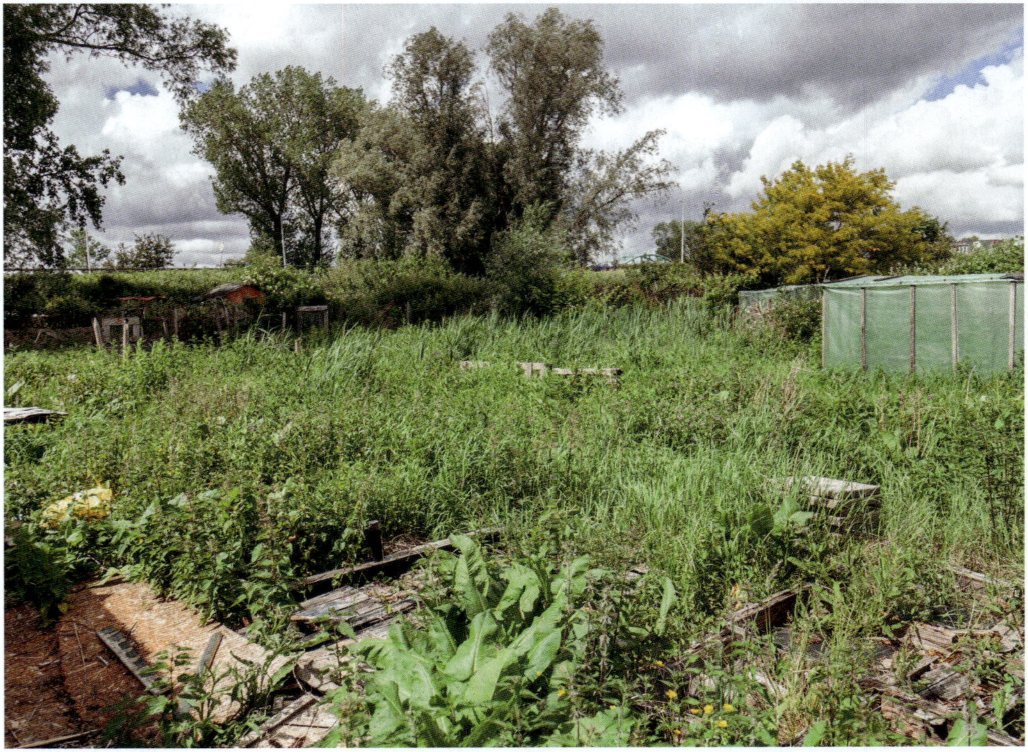

Stichting de Vrijbuiters (Plot on the corner of Bijlmerringkade and Provinciale weg, 1103 SB, Amsterdam)
In 2007, this allotment-garden community found one hectare of vacant land on the green field of Bijlmerweide in Amsterdam Zuidoost. When a private investor bought the terrain in 2020, the gardeners' rental agreement was not renewed. Since then, the garden sheds have been left to fend for themselves until the plans for a new building project have been decided.

These photos are part of a project about the content and language of judicial legislation that repeadetly fails to protect local life forms from being displaced in the name of privatisation and gentrification. The book *Cases of Withering Property* documents a variety of gardens in Amsterdam that will have to make way for other types of land use.

I myself don't think about which tree species are in my neighbourhood or how old they are. Cutting down trees means that it can take generations before the same atmosphere and ecosystem is created in your neighbour-

Goudberk (Golden birch) (1985)
Betula ermanii 'Holland'
Waterlandpleinbuurt

Iep (Elm) (1970)
Ulmus hollandica 'Vegeta'
Het breed

Vlier (Elderberry) (aangewaaid) (blown in)
Sambucus
Skate Café

Populier (Poplar) (1950)
Populus nigra 'Italica'
Nieuwendam

Es (Ash) (1940)
Fraxinus angustifolia
Noorderpark

Grauwe Abeel (Gray Abel) (1990)
Populus canescens 'De Moffart'
Schellingwouderbreek

Krimlinde (Crimean lime) (1990)
Tilia europaea 'Euchlora'
Buikslotermeerpark

Treurwilg (Weeping willow) (1975)
Salix sepulcralis 'Chrysocoma'
Nieuwendam

Kaukasische Vleugelnoot (Caucasian Wingnut)
(2010) *Pterocarya fraxinifolia*
Vliegenbos

hood. By portraying the trees in my neighbourhood, I hope to make them recognisable to fellow residents. Maybe we will resist their felling more quickly if we get to know the trees along with their names and ages?

Amerikaanse Linde (American Linden) (1967) *Tilia americana* Nieuwendam

Japanse Sierkers (Japanese Ornamental Cherry) (1980) *Prunus serrulata 'Kanzan'* Nieuwendam

Monumentaaliep (Monumental Elm) (1975) *Ulmus minor 'Sarniensis'* Tuindorp Vogeldorp

Gewonen Es (Plain Ash) (1952) *Fraxinus excelsior 'Allgold'* Waterlandpleinbuurt

Zoete Kers (Sweet Cherry) (1980) *Prunus avium* Buikslotermeerpark

Hollandse Iep (Dutch Elm) (1941–2021) R.I.P. *Ulmus hollandica 'Belgica'* Noorderpark

Amerikaans Krentenboompje (American Currant Tree) (2012) *Amelanchier lamarckii* Baanakkerspark

Schietwilg (White Willow) (2012) *Salix alba 'Chermesina'* Buikslotermeerpark

Treurwilg (Weeping Willow) (1950) *Salix sepulcralis 'Chrysocoma'* Noorderpark

Dizzy plants	Enjoying friends	Wedding dress
Hide and seek	It looks delicious	Playful paradise
Insect landing	Natural freedom	My mother's love
Never forgotten	Castle in the air	Powerperfume

Sun worshipper	Wonderful spirit	Jewellery
Bumblebee dance bath	Mother of all	Happy fun
Absolute beauty	Family beauty	Fashionable
Leonardo	Musical	Tears of love

I live on the Oude Nieuwstraat, in the middle of the constant stream of tourists. Sometimes it takes weeks before the street is swept clean. The police never walk through here. The residents, the owners of the prostitute's windows, and the sex workers all feel responsible for the area. It's a high-maintenance undertaking, and we often have to sweep the street ourselves. It is a cheerful place with lots of trees and plants, and a little mutual supervision among

old and young residents, old and young workers, and their customers. Now that those Airbnbs are gone, we see fewer tourists and less piss, puke, and drug dealing. With more permanent residents comes more responsibility. It won't all be up to us.

In Amsterdam Noord, residents often place their own benches, barbecues, flower pots, slides, or trampolines in the public space in front of their homes. But do all passersby feel welcome to stop and relax on these benches, or is this an appropriation of public space for personal use?

MOULIN ROUGE
Erotic Nightclub
86
Entrance around
WE LIVE HERE
Welkom
health check center
health check center
64

Fountains with free, clean drinking water can be found in the parks of Amsterdam. The water tastes much better than the water you can buy in the shops. Besides, it provides users of Amsterdam with their basic needs, which is especially important when access to drinking water is not a given.

Domela Nieuwenhuisplantsoen

Oosterpark

Wertheimpark

Sarphatipark

Vondelpark

Westerpark

Vondelpark

Oosterpark

If everyone spoke and understood everything in exactly the same way, then we would be living a monotonous life. There is still hope in Noord, where we Noorderlingen encounter confusion on every street corner. Whether they are on purpose, unintentional, touching, hilarious, or democratic, these instances are, above all, hopeful.

There is still real work going on here. On your heart, on your cross, on everything.

Bep van Klaveren was a celebrity, but a Rotterdammer. This is a very fine street, but can we really call it a boulevard?

A sign dictates that you can walk straight ahead, in a street where you could already walk straight ahead.

Read the other sign to figure it out.

Who is this footpath for?
A man and a clipped seahorse?

Confusion on the street.
Not everyone can handle it.

390 apartments under construction, for Noorderlingen of all shapes and sizes, built by only Dutch surnames.

Here's forward-looking governing for you. There may be no building yet, nor a parking lot, but the parking kiosk stands ready to take your money.

A street's 'furniture' is often terrifyingly uniform. But not in Noord! This is a showcase of varying models of street lamps, side by side.

What should we believe?

No misunderstanding possible. On this street, the population lives strictly segregated.

Floradorp stands in solidarity, even with the queers from Friesland.

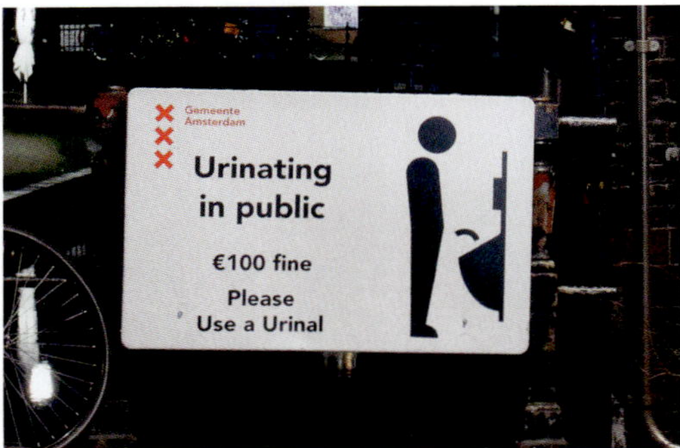
Gemeente
Amsterdam
Urinating
in public
€100 fine
Please
Use a Urinal

Gemeente
Amsterdam
Wild-
plassen
€100 boete

Gemeente
Amsterdam
No
Alcohol
Zone
€100 fine
Please
Drink Inside

Gemeente
Amsterdam
GEEN LAWAAI
OP HET WATER
BOETE €140

Gemeente
Amsterdam
Gemeente
Amsterdam
No Alcohol Zone
Wildplassen
€100 boete
€100 boete
Drink binnen
HS

Verboden te voeren
Art 5.18 APV

FINE: €150
Gemeente
Amsterdam

Gemeente
Amsterdam
Woon
buurt
Wees
alsjeblieft
stil
zzz

Ook voor u geldt: zet geen
afval naast de container.
U riskeert een boete
van minimaal € 95,-

I.v.m. markt op
vrijdag en zondag
geen objecten
plaatsen, deze zullen
worden verwijderd!

rookvrij

21.00 - 08.00 h

Voetgangers op
de rijbaan.
Geef elkaar de ruimte.
amsterdam.nl/corona

fietsstraat
auto te gast
Maak ruimte
voor elkaar

Eva Bollen, Isa van Bossé
BULKY WASTE DISPOSAL

In the old neighbourhoods of Noord, you need a 'household waste card' to throw away your waste, while this formality is not necessary in the new housing estates. Information about waste disposal from the municipality to residents is unclear: residents are not informed how to apply for the household waste card, only two cards are

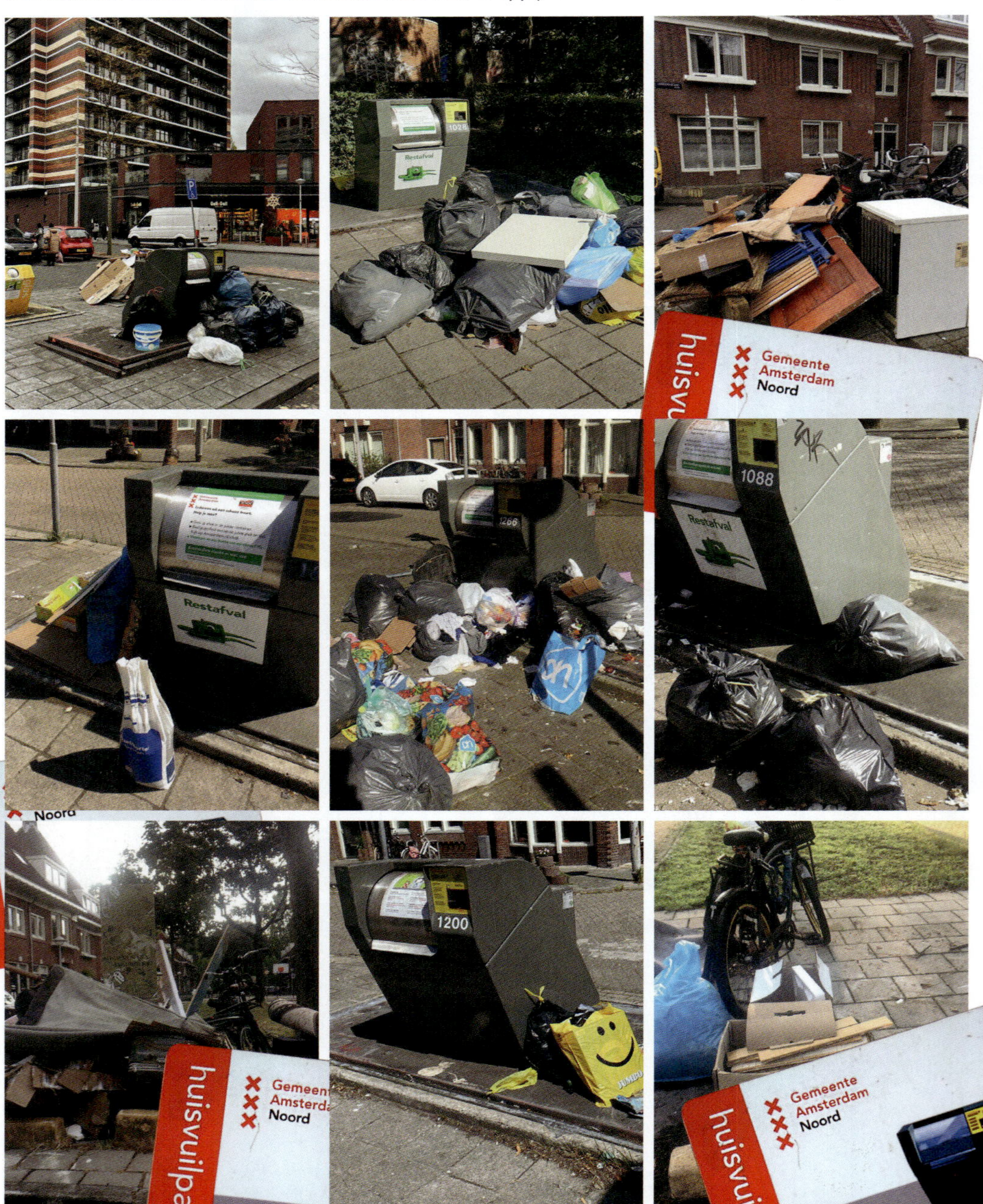

available per address, and language presents a barrier. These disparities in the waste disposal-process give the misleading impression that new housing estates are inhabited by cleaner people.

Matilda Médard
CYCLISTS, MOBILISE!

As a cycling city, the bicycle traffic lights in Amsterdam form an arena for activism: the poles are full of self-made stickers with political or playful messages, self-promotion, or messages that encourage action.

As a democratic means of transport, the bicycle is used by Amsterdammers of all persuasions, and the short waiting period for a traffic light is a spontaneous moment of social reflection.

Layla Gijsen
SWAP ME!

The average Amsterdammer knows how to maintain their bicycle. But since the emergence of bicycle subscriptions such as Swapfiets, the bicycle has become an interchangeable object. The city has turned into a sea of blue front wheels. Monoculture is at its peak. Join us and flip a swap bike to take a stand against

monoculture, because *herkenning is de beste erkenning*. So go out into the street. Within ten seconds, you will find a Swapfiets. Turn it over, and *klaar is Kees*!

This photo series was made in forty-five minutes and gives a good impression of the obstacles I encounter when I manoeuvre through Amsterdam in my wheelchair. Because the sidewalks are not very spacious, they quickly fill up with incorrectly parked bicycles, scaffolding, and other obstacles.

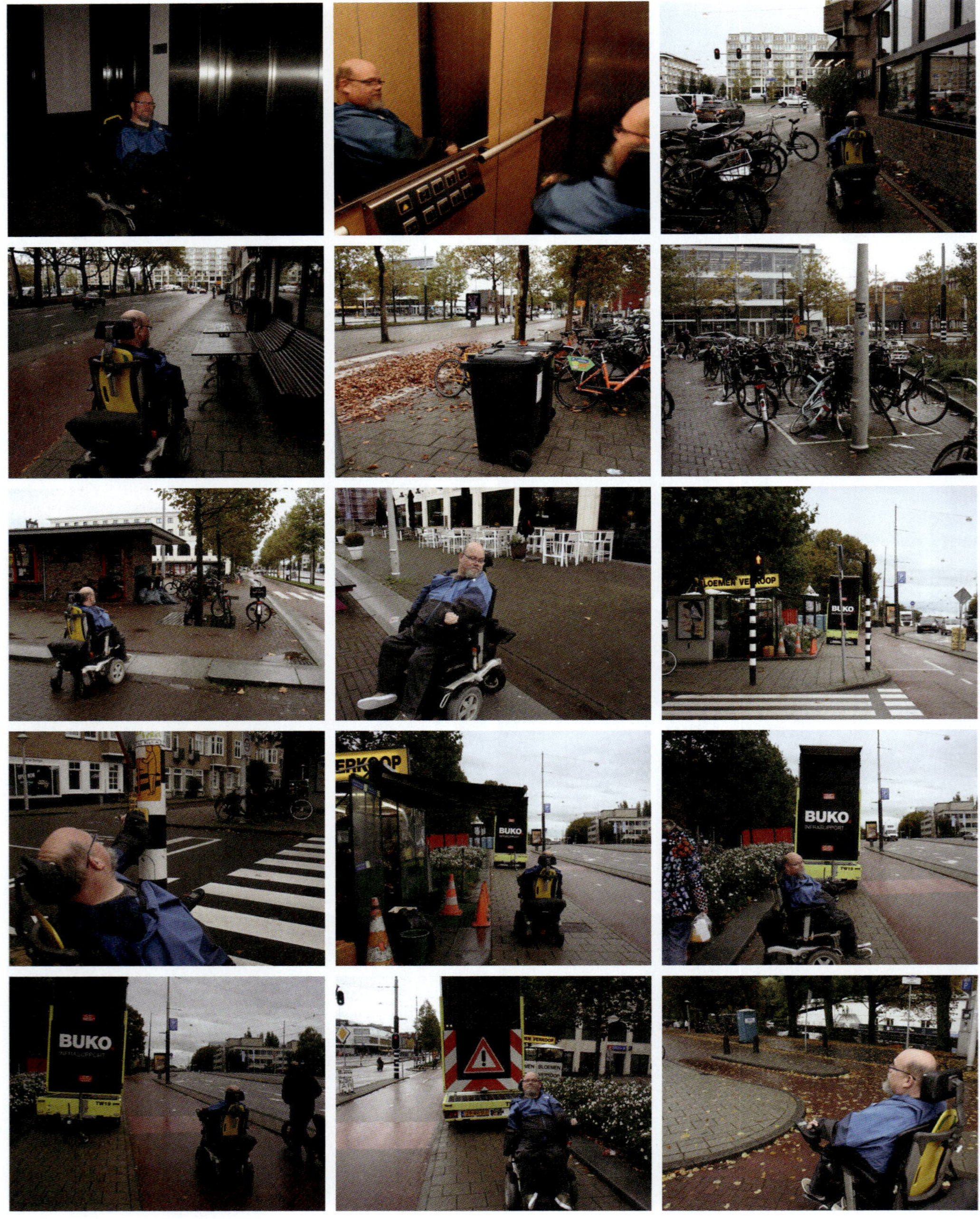

There are also few ramps. Participating is not always easy in Amsterdam, and that's why I don't always feel welcome. Smarter design and a little more awareness in how we deal with the built environment is for everyone!

In the 1950s, when there was a great housing shortage in Amsterdam, houseboats became a permanent part of the cityscape. The city now has the largest concentration of houseboats in the Netherlands, with almost 3,000 berths. There are three different types of houseboat: *schepen*, *scharken*, and *arken*.

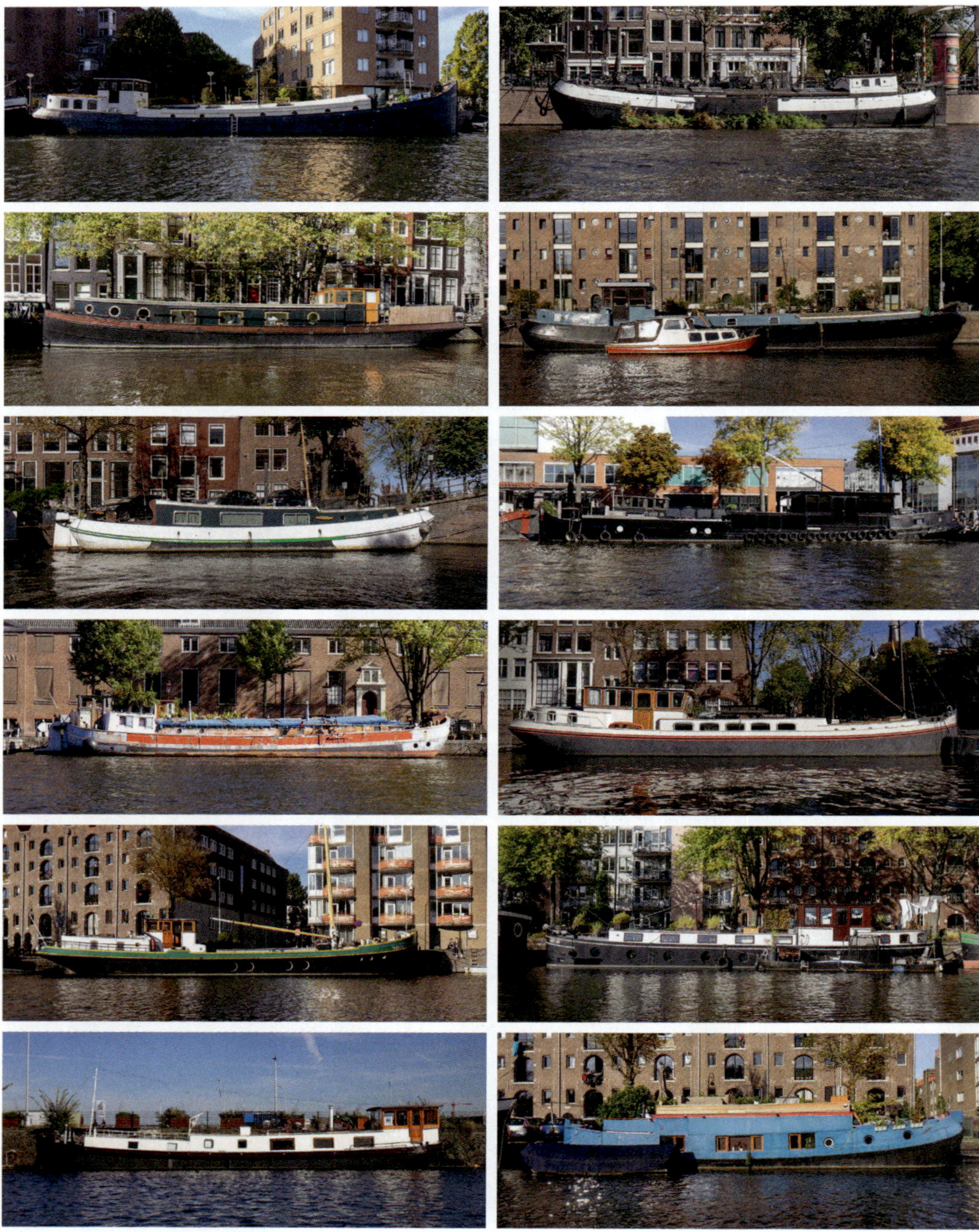

Schepen are often decommissioned inland vessels or otherwise historic ships that have been given a residential function. Sometimes these houseboats are still able to sail.

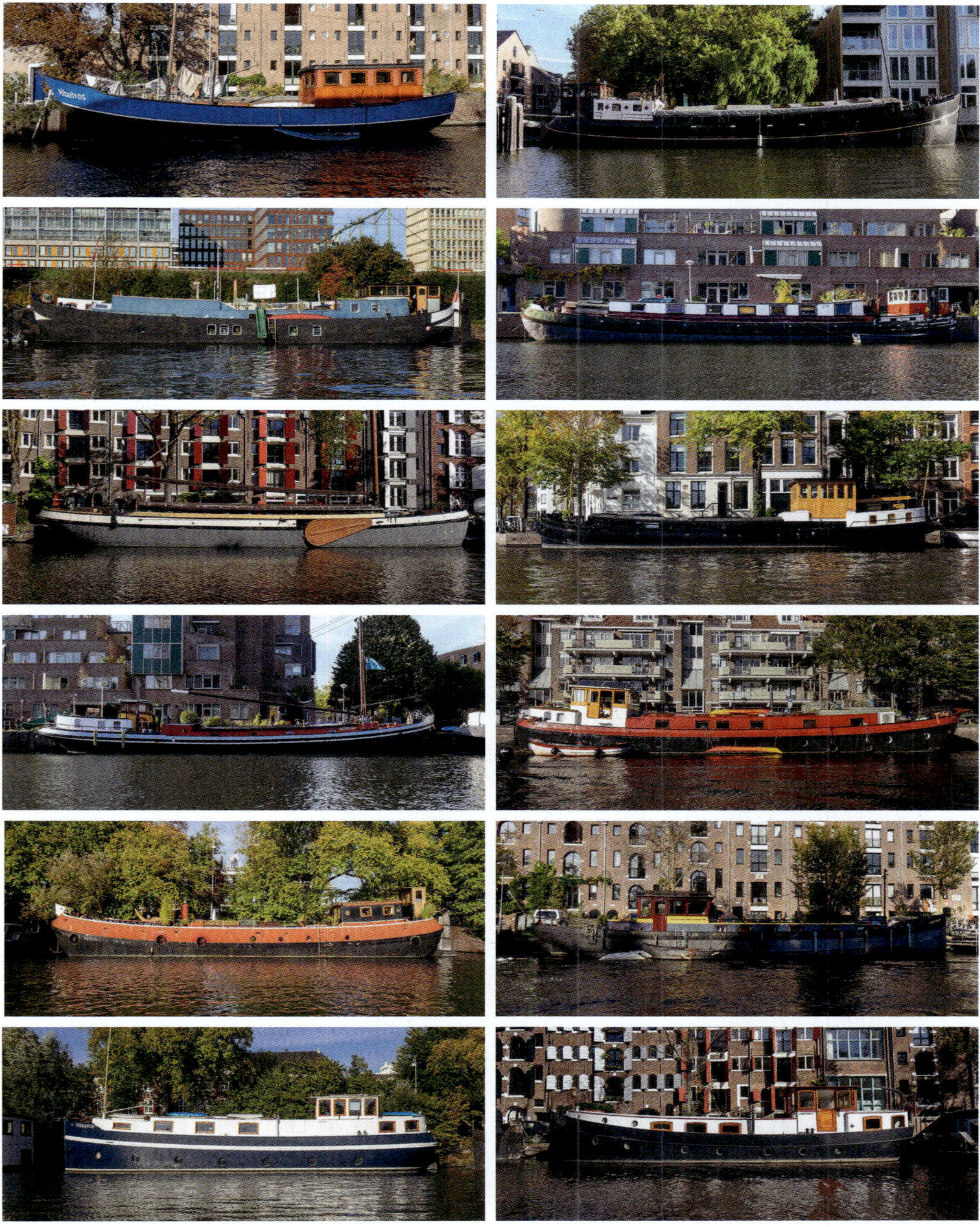

A schark is a decommissioned inland vessel on which a wooden, stone, or plastic superstructure has been made. A schark resembles an ark, but it is distinguished by its steel substructure.

An ark consists of a concrete box on which a wooden, stone, or plastic construction is made. Marco and his sons Wouter and Job designed and built their own houseboat, De Cornelis (bottom right).

Once upon a time, I wandered, meandered, and slithered here. The canals they call Amsterdam were once the endless wetlands, muddy streams, and free-flowing rivers where I found my home. Now, I find deafening underwater noise, dams impossible to overcome, and water that tastes so bad it must be unearthly.

I am Anguilla Anguilla, a.k.a. the eel. Still I migrate over six thousand kilometers to get here. Threatened with extinction, at least let me tell you my story. A story that has as much value to humans as it does to myself.

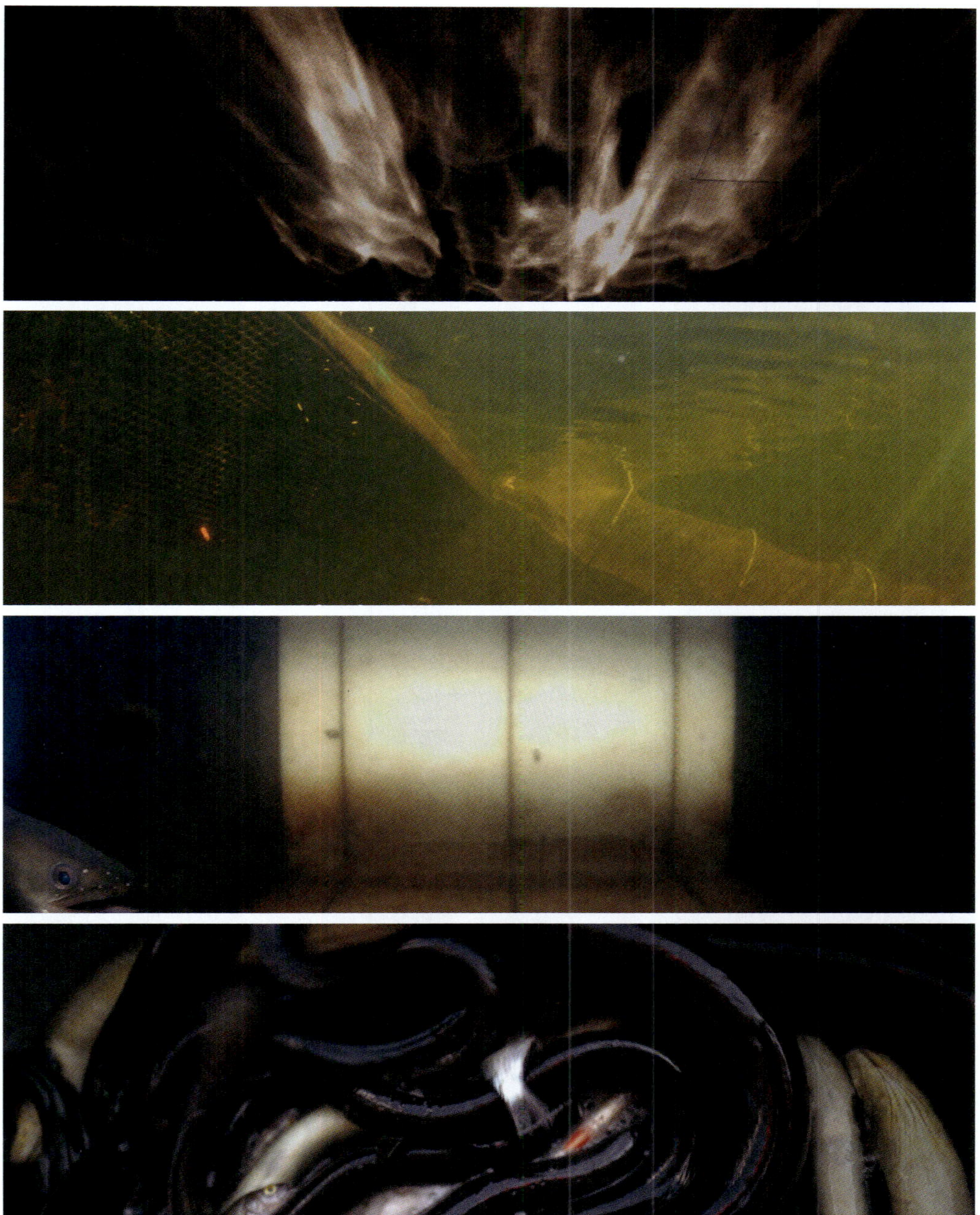

Mateo Vega, Maxime Garcia Diaz, Sam Broekman

EQUINIX AM3/AM4

Amsterdam Science Park is a key site in the history of the internet, having hosted one of the first connections outside the US and functioning as a major node for global traffic through the Amsterdam Internet Exchange

(AMS-IX). The Equinix AM3/AM4 data centre is home to countless Big Tech servers, and one of the most visible sites of Amsterdam's expansive, often invisible, digital infrastructure.

Being interested in transitional and negative spaces over the years, I visually archive the northern neighbourhood NDSM, juxtaposing different levels of detail in the documentation.

Zooming in and out from the same perspective, I archive intimate details from an almost-lost cultural European epicentre.

As a born and bred Noorderling, I have been seeing my district change for years, and at a rapid pace in recent times. I try to keep track of time with my camera. These are places I visited as a little girl and that I have taken

for granted for so long. These places are so commonplace that few people take the time to appreciate them, but I'm not sure for how long they will continue to exist.

Qusai Alsaify, Saja Amro, Farah Fayad, Ayman Hassan, Ott Metusala, Samira Vogel

SCANNING THE CITY

While we were new to the city that was in lockdown, designer Huda Smitshuizen-AbuFares invited us to direct our gaze to a part of the city where we had not yet been.

Diamantbuurt, Saffierstraat *Outer side*

Dappermarkt, Commelingstraat *South side*

Dappermarkt, Commelingstraat *North side*

Docklands, Oostelijke Handelskade

Docklands, Stuurmankade

Docklands, Zeeburgerkade, *former Eastern Docklands warehouses transformed into apartments ...*

... with a beautiful location on the water

Diamantbuurt, Saffierstraat *Inner side*

Eeke Brussee

BUILT ON SLAVERY

One might not realise that many of the historical buildings in the centre of Amsterdam are closely connected to the Dutch slave trade. These buildings are some of the locations where Dutch people made decisions over other people's lives. These decisions materialised in the trade of enslaved (African) people, and further involvement in the transatlantic trade.

Amstel 87, residency of Jacob Rühle (1751–1828),
an influential official within the Dutch West India Company (WIC) and trader of enslaved people.

Herengracht 502, residency of Paulus Godin, administrator of the WIC and director of the Society of Suriname.
Today, it is the official residence of the mayor.

Although these buildings often form the backdrop of tourist photographs and are commonly referred to as heritage from 'the Golden Age' (a common reference to the seventeenth century), I find it important to stress how the history of slavery is ingrained in the Dutch built environment, and to emphasise how present this past actually remains, especially since systemic racism continues to be very present in Dutch society.

Keizersgracht 442–448, firm Hope & Co. Thomas Hope was administrator of the WIC and VOC (Dutch East India Company). The firm also lent money to plantations in the West Indies, facilitating the slave trade in several ways. The company traded goods on the coast of Angola for enslaved Africans to be taken to Port au Prince (Haiti) for further trade.

Oudezijds Voorburgswal 195–199, Dutch West India Company. The WIC held exclusive rights to trade with all countries in Africa and the Americas. The WIC commissioned Johan Maurits to conquer the coast of Brazil and Fort Elmina in Ghana. Money that was generated was then invested in the built environment.

Sources: Amsterdam – Mapping Slavery. (z.d.). www.mappingslavery.nl/kaarten-2/kaarten-nederland/amsterdam. Sporen van Slavernij in Amsterdam: particulieren en ondernemers. (z.d.). www.digitaleetalages.nl/thema/amsterdam/amsterdam-en-de-slavernij/sporen-van-slavernij-in-amsterdam--particulieren-en-ondernemers.

Amstel 87, residency of Jacob Rühle (1751–1828). Influential official within the WIC and trader of enslaved people.

Herengracht 464, these properties were owned by the firm Van Eeghen & Co.
From 1672 to 1770, the family business Van Eeghen & Co traded in West Indian products.

Binnengasthuisstraat 9, auction site for art and real estate. Caribbean plantations including enslaved people were also regularly offered for sale. In the inventory, it is possible to check exactly which enslaved people were bought: and see the names, occupations, and monetary value assigned to them.

Nieuwezijds Voorburgwal 147, in 1683, the Society of Suriname was founded. Their aim was to exploit Suriname as a settlement. The board of the Society, the 'directors', met every first Wednesday of the month at the Paleis op de Dam.

Joséphine Dupuy d'Angeac
A VILLAGE WITHIN THE CITY

Cultural free spaces are becoming increasingly rare in Amsterdam. Illegally squatted buildings provide a stage for the free expression of subculture, which forms from the bottom up. Sporadically, these sanctuaries live on as legalised, cultural organisations, but most of the time their inhabitants are evicted. This collection of current and past squats brings together places that have shaped my relationship with Amsterdam and its residents. Despite its versatility, the squatting scene is a close-knit network. If you're part of the scene, it feels like a small village spread out over a big city. The question is whether counterculture can really be celebrated in this city?

Het Slangenpand
Squatted in late 1970
and vacated in March 2015

OCCII
Squatted in 1982
and legalised in 1992

Vrankrijk
Squatted November 1982
and legalised in 1992

OT301
Squatted in 1999
and collectively owned since 2006

ADM
Squatted in 1997, evicted and
moved to ADM Noord in January 2019

Voorwaarts
Informal anti-squat,
the beginning of Radio
Voorwaarts and a free
adventure 2014–2017

Joe's Garage
First squatted in Pretoriustraat 28
from February 2001 to October
2008. Since September 2005,
it's a squat in Pretoriusstraat 43

Anjelierstraat
Squatted by the Kinderen van Mokum
(Children of Mokum) from April to June 2018

Het Klokhuis
Squatted by Kinderen van Mokum
from September 2018 to April 2021

Mobiele-eenheid
Squatted from October 2018
to February 2019

Bowlwerk
Squatted in March 2016,
now threatened with eviction

Keizer
Re-squatted since July 2020

Hotel Mokum
Squatted by Pak Mokum Terug
from October to November 2021

Stomerij Nicole
Squatted by Mokum Kraakt
in March 2022

SQUATTING BECOMES | PROHIBITED BY LAW

JOE'S GARAGE
ADM
OCCII
VRANKRIJK
HET SLANGENPAND
OT301

Voorwaa. M H
A KEIZ.
KLOKH. Nic.

1980 1981 1982 1983 1984 1985 1986 1987 1988 1989 1990 1991 1992 1993 1994 1995 1996 1997 1998 1999 2000 2001 2002 2003 2004 2005 2006 2007 2008 2009 2010 2011 2012 2013 2014 2015 2016 2017 2018 2020 2020 2021 2022 2023

YOU CAN'T EVICT OUR IDEALS

Although Amsterdam used to be known as a rebellious city, where squats paved the way for the rich cultural programmes of former squats like Paradiso and the Melkweg, the strict ban on squatting and tough enforcement have resulted in a lack of truly free spaces. Renamed Hotel Mokum, the vacant hotel on Marnixstraat was squatted at the end of 2021. The building was in a state of disrepair. We cleaned, renovated, repaired the floors, and made furniture. We received many positive comments and support from the local residents, who felt that we improved the quality of the neighbourhood with the activities we organised.

Hotel Marnix
Until May 2019

Two years of vacancy
June 2019–October 2021

We reappropriated this neglected private space as public. Part of the building was used for housing, the rest for political and cultural events and meetings between different groups of people. In the six weeks of Hotel Mokum's existence, we organised a chess tournament, a textile-printing company, an exhibition with more than sixty artists, two political debate evenings, three film evenings, and ten evenings for drinks. The ad-hoc events on art, culture, and activism that we organised reached more than 400 visitors each week.

Hotel Mokum
16 October–27 November, 2021,
receiving more than 400 visitors a week for
art, culture, and activism

Vacant again
Since 28 November, 2021

These are some of the places and buildings that have been squatted by the refugee-collective We Are Here between 2012 and 2020. Some places and buildings that the collective occupied have transformed completely by now, others are currently in use, and others are still vacant.

Notweg

Erik de Roodestraat 14

Weteringschans 109

Havenstraat 6

Kralenbeek 100

Linnaeushof 4

Jan Tooropstraat 649

Nieuwe Kerkstraat 157

Keienbergweg 8

Pieter Calandlaan 1

Nienoord 2

Joan Muyskenweg 32a

Reigersbos 33

Rudolf Dieselstraat

Meester G. Groen van Prinsterelaan 114

Van de Sande Bakhuijzenstraat 2

Entrada 60C

Garage Kempering

Bijlmerdreef 588

Willem Fenengastraat 15

Jan Tooropstraat 29

Zuidelijke Wandelweg 30

Dapperstraat 315

Bijlmerdreef 1141a

The cosy, comfortable surface of Amsterdam overrules the concerns of its inhabitants, which are often pushed aside. However, they bubble back up like mushrooms in the form of subtle rebellion in the streets, in the form of stickers, posters, tags, or affirmations. Critiques of structural racism, capitalism, the fear of the climate crisis,

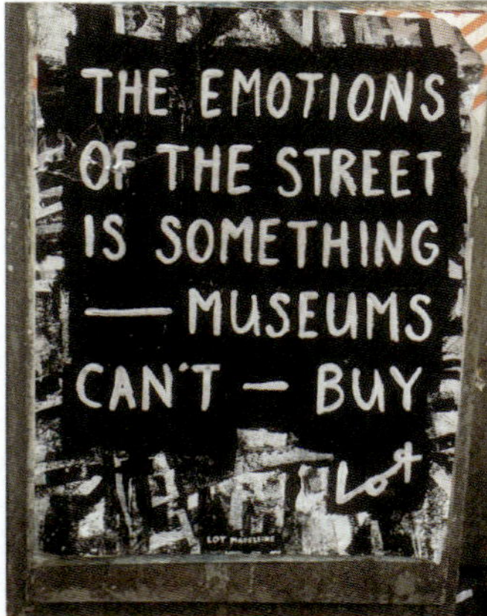

possible vaccine mandates, and more are taken to the clean comfort of Amsterdam's streets. Temporary yet thought-provoking.

We are an artists' collective consisting of people who have come to the Netherlands as refugees. The collective originated from the activist movement We Are Here, in which we as refugees drew attention to our hopeless situation.

we are here
Wij zijn hier 24/7 !

NO TEMPORY SOLUTION
PERMANENT
RESIDENCY

WE WANT A
NORMAL LiFE

GIVE US
PERMiSSiON
TO STAY !
REMOVE ouR FINGERPRINT

Geen vluchteling op
straat
We Are Here
We Are Here
We Are Here

FREDOM
FoR ALL
REFUGEES

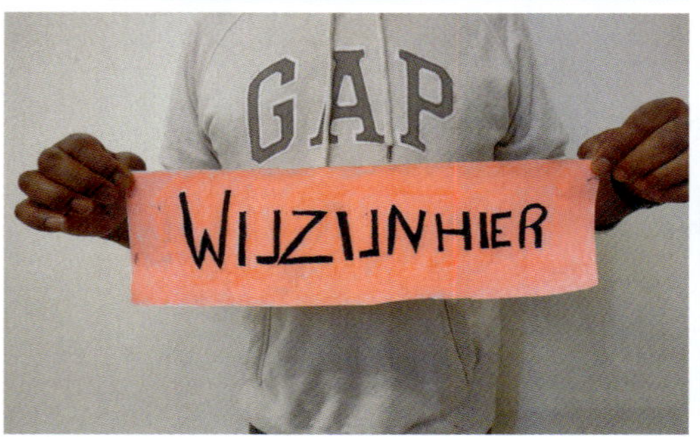
GAP
WIJ ZIJN HIER

Amsterdam
WE HERE
ARE

Struggling to find a place to live is a downside of living in Amsterdam. The city drives young people outside its edges, or forces them to accept a temporary solution with few or no rights. The unregistered addresses (in red) were more affordable, while the official places I could only move in after securing a higher-paying job.

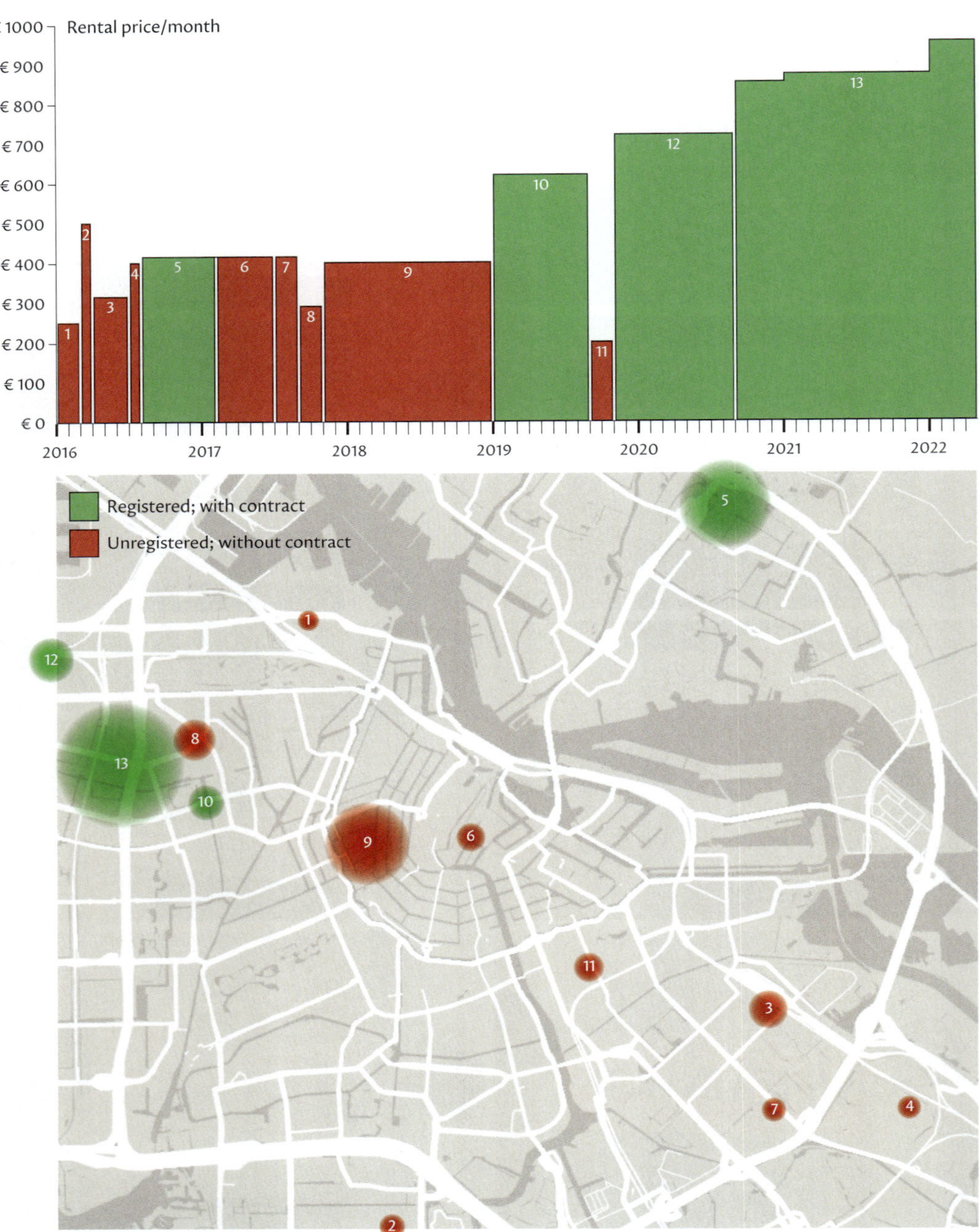

Yuri Veerman
YOU'RE TOO LATE

Average house price in Amsterdam (statistics from CBS and o ficial Land Registry)
from 1995 to the first quarter of 2021.

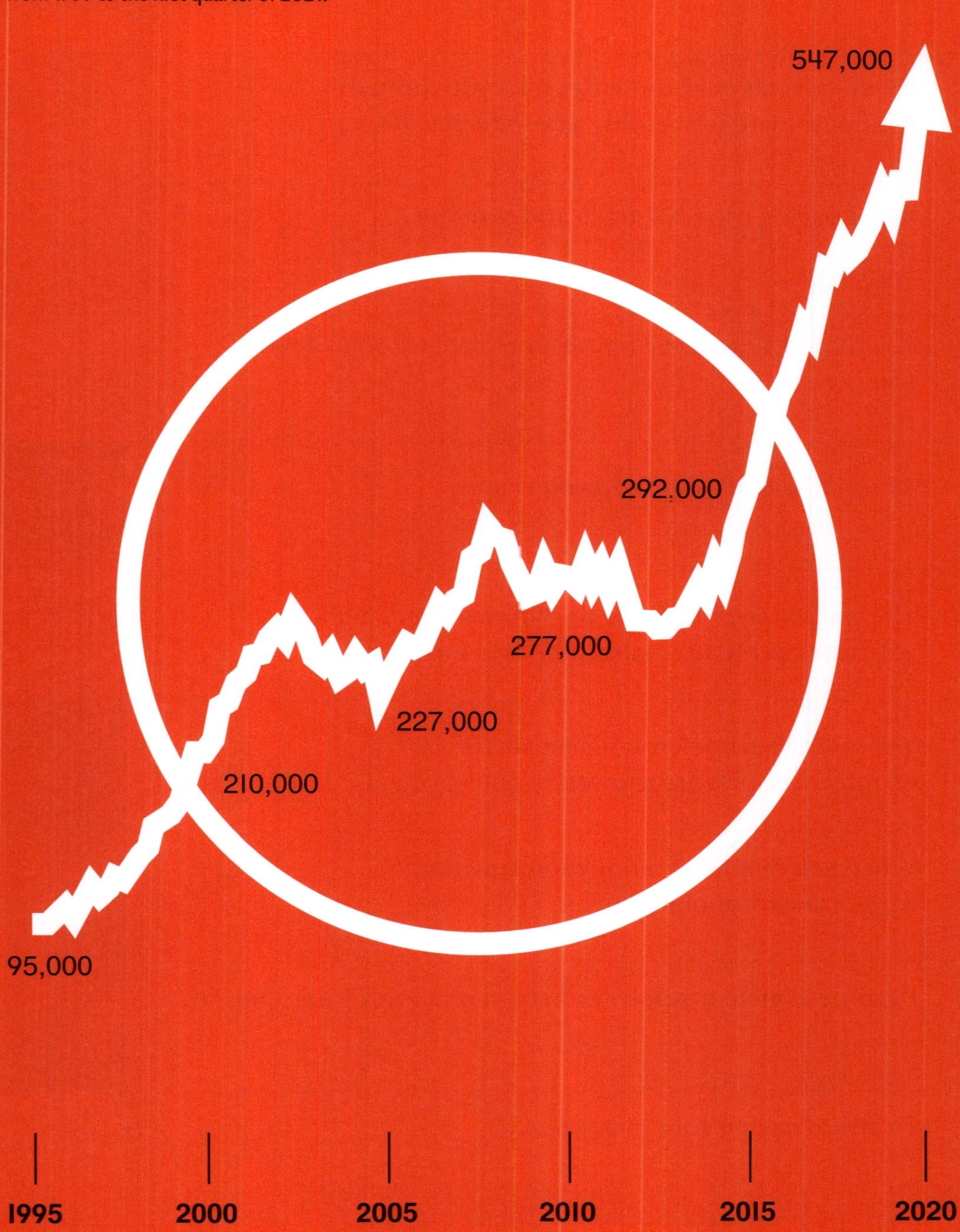

Connect the sentences together to find the best tips out there!

When the cult of housemates puts you through the housemate trial during a *hospiteeravond*, you …

Avoid paying the €332 trash and taxes by …

You rented a room in a house where pets aren't allowed, you …

Afford to pay all your *belastingen* by …

The walls in the house are so thin that every night you hear your housemates snoring, you …

You saw a Facebook room post where no internationals are allowed to apply, you …

When you're renting a 6m^2 room and tend to get claustrophobic, you …

Become eligible to apply for a room that is for 'Girls Only' by …

To afford paying your rent, you …

	… trip on some LSD and imagine the walls melting.
	… by adopting the zero-waste lifestyle.
	… start meowing every time your landlord shows up to block out your dog's barking.
	… become eligible to apply for it.
	… replace your Facebook profile picture with a *hagelslag* portrait of you to prove your Dutchness.
	… asking the person with the room ad on Facebook to change it to 'no preference'.
	… impress them by frying up some delicious homemade vegan *bitterballen*.
	… stealing the stolen bikes and selling them off to your customers.
	… snore even louder to assert dominance.

On a journey admiring the details of Amsterdam's buildings, some elements were missing from the façades that I knew before moving from Beirut, but then again others I found felt very much familiar.

This curation of windows is an homage to the explicit sex-work architecture of Amsterdam, in an effort to analyse and preserve them in all their truth. The attention shifts to the architectural decor, which surrounds the usual protagonists. Details of alarm systems, closed-circuit cameras, and window-pane spikes contrast with the intimacy of soft white lace curtains and glowing red lanterns. Constant surveillance of the body in the public realm, a daily fight for anonymity and visibility.

Today, a climate of uncertainty reigns over the streets of De Wallen. The area has, over the years, been the target of drastic municipality initiatives, aiming to clean the centre of its characteristic grittiness. The sex workers have been excluded from the conversation. Some workers have turned to working from home, sometimes in unsuitable or even unsafe working conditions. What will become of De Wallen's windows? And most importantly, what will become of the workers behind them?

When we pass by the massage parlours in the city, look at the red led light boxes that say 'Welcome' or the portraits of Buddha and lucky cats that keep beckoning. Whether it's a Thai massage or a Chinese one, their decoration style is consistent. Sometimes, we look at massage salons with the old stereotypeing mindset regarding ethnic but also gender backgrounds, seeing them as symbolic of the porn industry. Are you a male consumer or a patient who needs special pain treatment? Most of the workers need to learn Chinese

acupuncture and human meridians and even gain certificates before they can open massage parlours. Some of the women came here illegally, many of them found a Dutch husband, all of them worked hard to get a permanent residence card. They worked legally to integrate into Dutch society with their own hands and sweat to find a prosperous future in the Netherlands. Now this industry is gradually becoming transparent and legalised.

Lou de Monchy, Deniz Aktaş
WINDOW DISPLAYS

I often went after school as a child to the Jordaan neighbourhood, where youngsters are treated to many colourful and funny displays in people's windows. Objects behind the glass often serve to block pedestrians' view inside the home, while the residents festively display their trinkets to the outside world. Now that I am

olbut, I find this captures the contrast between cultural openness and closedness, which is typically Dutch. The large windows at eye level suggest an openness and tolerance for the other, but on closer inspection this turns out to be a façade. Which objects are used?

Architecture is a manifestation of culture: it reflects ideology, belief systems, governance, social order, and identity. In this day and age, where we see a heightened emphasis on group identity, I can't resist inquiring as to

whether we are genuinely able to coexist and tolerate each other, or not? Are we prepared to accept that what we see in our salient landscape reflects the content of our consciousness?

The Municipality of Amsterdam and two social housing corporations, De Key and Eigen Haard, developed the residential complex Startblok Elzenhagen on Elzenhagen, a former athletic field in Amsterdam Noord. This complex provides accommodation for 540 young people, half of whom have a Dutch nationality, while the

other half of the residents have come to the Netherlands as refugees and have just received a residence permit as status holders. They are building their future here, together.

Adinda van Kranendonk
WHAT MAKES YOU FEEL AT HOME?

As residents of Startblok Elzenhagen, we come from all corners of the world and everyone has the same size flats at our disposal: 25 m² to furnish in our own way and make home. Home, the most important place in our

Mustafa (Baghdad, Iraq) 'I feel at home here because there is security. This is the place that gives me both that feeling and a sense of peace.'

Lisa (Groningen, Netherlands) 'The kitchen (a little small). There you can inhale the aromas of simply prepared food: pasta, grilled vegetables, and bread.'

David (Al Hasaka, Syria)
'Do I feel at home? I do not know.'

Moussa (Nielle, Ivory Coast) 'I am very happy with the size of my studio. It is functional and everything fits.'

life. How do my neighbours do that? Will they manage to feel at home in a place where they are only allowed to live temporarily?

Junia (Udonthani, Thailand) 'Peace and harmony ensure a sense of relaxation and coming home. But my house will never feel like home without my four-legged friend.'

Adam (Gaza, Palestine) 'I think it's home, so I feel it's home.'

Sam (Tehran, Iran) 'My stuff, furniture, the smell in my studio, the view, and the peace—if my neighbours allow it.'

Abdo (Aleppo, Syria) 'I feel safe here.'

Medina (Eritrea) 'I like having my own place.'

Mirjam (Amsterdam, Netherlands) 'My house is really my own nest. There are nice places to sit, I like to watch movies and play records here.'

Ahmed (Taiz, Yemen) 'Because it's my own place.'

Katrine (Syria) 'Safety and beauty.'

Nick (Ruurlo, Netherlands) 'At the top of the list, I would have to say that my bunny Nootje makes me feel at home.'

Jim (Amsterdam, Netherlands)
'My lights, music, and the food I make.'

Maria (Ruinerwold, Netherlands)
'The people and the pieces of greenery.'

Adinda (Zutphen, Netherlands)
'Here I can withdraw and I feel like Adinda.'

My house integrates differently shaped bodies. When I moved into my apartment in 1997, the intention was that I could live here comfortably with my body, at a height of 117 cm. With the help of family and an occupational therapist, the Municipality of Amsterdam developed a high-low kitchen that would fit perfectly into the existing kitchen. Thanks to the kitchen worktop being adjustable within a range of 60 cm, I can cook sitting

down without physical strain because everything is within reach, and also because the upper cabinets can adjust up and down along with it. In addition, my taller visitors can help me, for the pleasure of cooking together. Fifteen years ago, a necessary technical repair had unfortunately reduced the range by half, from 60 cm to 30 cm. But it still works!

Nadia Sbai, Peik Suyling, Tina Lenz i.s.m. Bakkerij de Eenvoud, Vrouw & Vaart

BAKING BODY STORIES

Various cultures live together in the western neighbourhood of Slotermeer. There, the Schakel community centre is a safe haven for everyone. Residents from Slotermeer and other parts of the Amsterdam Nieuw-West district wanted a neighbourhood oven to bake bread together. So every Tuesday, Bakkerij de Eenvoud fires the neighbourhood oven.

While making the dough, letting it rise, and baking, conversations about life in the neighbourhood also arise. On International Women's Day in 2022, forty women expressed themselves by kneading Fatima hands that symbolise support, patience, and defence against evil.

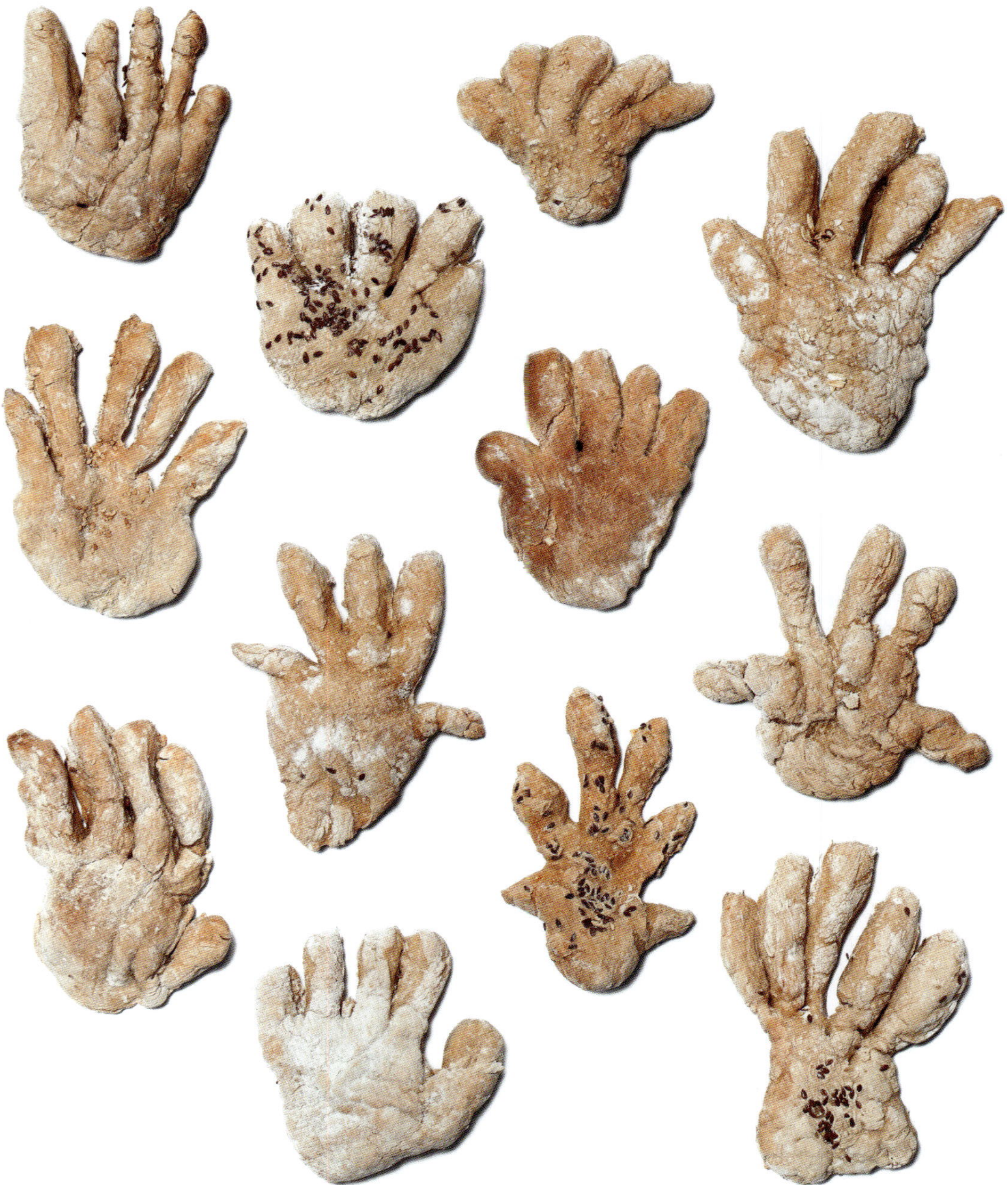

I organise neighbourhood dinners at Startblok Elzenhagen, where I discover the tastes and smells that emanate from under my neighbours' doors. These drawings are just a glimpse of the diverse culinary delights we prepare.

Poffertjes

Roselle flower, a variety of hibiscus

Roselle juice

Prosecco

Ramen tofu

Saffron ice

Ravioli
Cimi di Rape

Pomegranate

Kuku sabai
Herb omelette

Atheke

Cassave

Fried Fish

Rice, raw fish, seaweed

Prawn *Soy Sauce* **Sushi**

Kibbeh

Mozzarella

Figs

Stuffed Tomatoes
Rice

Pizza
Bacon, mushroom, pepperoni, mozzarella

Fig tart

Injera 'Shiro'
Beef, cabbage, beets, potatoes, peppers, tomatoes

Put the kettle on

Amsterdam is the city that really shaped me. It is the places and people close to me that form the city for me, and I feel most at home during the times spent with my friends. Amsterdam is a place where I feel the freedom to act how I want.

AIN'T
NOTHING.
LIKE IT

A10
Molenwijk
Kadoelen
MIJN HUUR WORDT TE DUUR
de ARK
Buiksloot
VERDEDIG NOORD
Tuindorp Oostzaan
blanke
Buikslo
IJ
Volewij
RED DE BOMEN
RED DE BOMEN
RED NOORD
Vogelbuu
IJplein

GROUPS FOR RESIDENTS

1. Verdedig Noord
2. Bewonerscommissie Voorsteven
3. Noordas
4. Buurtvaders
5. Stichting Arrahma
6. Bewonersplatform Vogelbuurt/IJplein
7. Stichting Red Amsterdam Noord
8. Actie Groep Elzo Amsterdam Noord
9. Vogelburinnenapp
10. Stichting Noorderpark

FORMAL COMMUNITY PARTNERS

11. Huis van de Wijk: Banne
12. Huis van de Wijk: De Evenaar
13. Huis van de Wijk: De Meeuw
14. Huis van de Wijk: Waterlandplein
15. A-Lab
16. Stichting !Woon
17. Buurthuis van Der Pek
18. Tolhuistuin
19. Modestraat

SPORTS

20. Boksschool the Big Lab
21. Northside Ballers
22. Rayaction
23. Share
24. Tamse Sport
25. Dat! School
- Spin Speeltuinen

INFORMAL CARETAKERS & FOOD INITIATIVES

26. Dream Sisters Noord
27. Florakokjes
28. Flora 4 Life
29. Moeders van Noord
30. Cezellig op stap met Linda
31. Adopteer een Peer
32. De Helpende Hand
33. Sonja Kookt
34. Helen's Free Food
35. Stichting Cleopatra
36. Stichting Malak
37. De Banne Hopper
38. Weggeefwinkel Tjalkstraat
39. Weggeefwinkel Bloemenbuurt
- Solidariteit Weggeef Kastjes

BUSINESSES

40. Mok Amsterdam
41. Snackbar 't Puntje
42. Colourful Goodies
43. Hebben en Houwen
44. Boka's
45. Ijskoud de Beste
46. Zucchini Amsterdam
47. Boekhandel van Noord
48. Boekhandel over het Water
49. JJ's Bizz
50. Arra de Barber
51. Robin Kapitein
52. Fruit en Nootjes
53. De Lokatie
54. De Gele Pomp
55. De Roze Tanker
56. De VerbroederIJ

During the two years of the pandemic, witnessing empty streets and spaces shutting down, I started questioning the ethics of private economic growth versus social growth. I still believe that there is—now more than ever—a need and urgency to collectively generate alternative economies initiated and locally run by citizens. Let's start by appreciating the spaces already embedded in our urban fabric. They may currently be overshadowed again by the masses of tourists and the commercial activities tailored to their desires. But let's not forget them, as our simple and continuous presence in these spaces—meeting a friend over a drink—has the potential to empower the (trans)formation of the city.

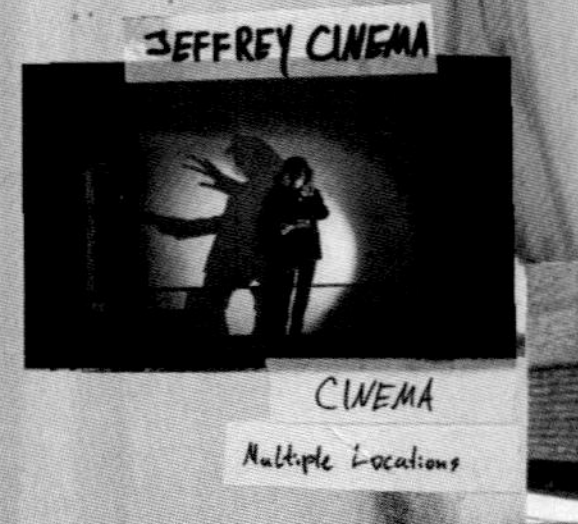

CINEMA

Multiple Locations

CINEMA

Van Hallstraat 52-1

SQUAT/CULTURAL
POLITICAL CENTER

Kinkerstraat 304

ART

WG Plein Ho nr 80

SQUAT/CULTURAL
POLITICAL EVENTS

Marnixstraat 382

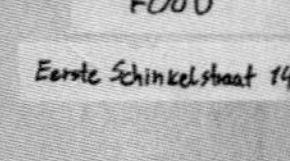

FOOD

Eerste Schinkelstraat 14

MUSIC/ART
CULTURAL CENTER

Overtoom 301

MUSIC/CULTURAL
CENTER

Vondelpark 8A

BAR/ART

Karperweg 45

This map is a starting point to rethink economies as sites of ethical action and solidarity; as platforms through which we can share resources, break free of mundane expectations of the future city, and explore reflective imagination. The map focuses on the communal and cultural spaces of entertainment that I visit. It provides an invitation to remember the alternative economies around us, and to choose what kind of economy we want to contribute to. Here are captivating alternatives to business as usual.

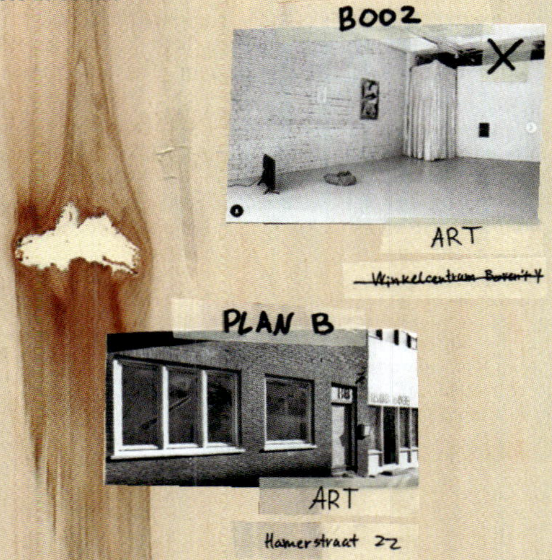

ART

Winkelcentrum Boven't Y

ART

Warmoesstraat 139

PLAN B

ART

Hamerstraat 22

ART

Vijzelgracht 21

CINEMA / BAR

Roetersstraat 170

BAR / CULTURAL CENTER

ART

Magersfonteinstraat 12

For trans and gender diverse people, such as gender nonconforming, nonbinary, drag queens, and transgender people who are, too conspicuous (perhaps because they do not seem cisgender enough), there is no place that is inherently safe. Verbal and physical violence, exclusion, weird looks, and unkind reactions are common, so places can be perceived as threatening.

Safety is subjective but less so the further you fall outside of the cisgender image. The problems are intersectional, as are the injustices we suffer. This chart is based on my experiences as an older, white, gender-nonconforming trans punk, with the experiences of the wider community in mind.

The graph progresses from generally unsafe and unfriendly places on the left (in red), to increasingly safe places on the right (in green). Not all unsafe places are always so: people can still go to a clothing store and not experience any problems, or receive good assistance from the police. To indicate this, these organisations get a dash of green. Likewise, not all safe places are safe or pleasant for everyone, which is why you'll see a dash of red under the safe places. That does not alter the fact that it's never pleasant anywhere if people behave in a racist or sexist way ...

*Trans stands for the whole community, from those who knew they were like this at the age of three to those who only confessed it on their deathbed. From those who radically adapt their bodies to those where nothing is visible and are tacitly accepted, such as the jazz musician Billy Tipton.

Suit supply
For queers and non cis-passing trans people, this is one nasty clothing store. If you seem too much of the 'opposite sex' they will force you to go to another store.

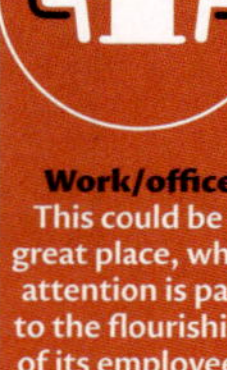

Straight bar
(a normal bar)
If you stand out as a trans person, it can be very unpleasant to be there, especially on weekends and by the end of the evening. You're better off going to Saarein, Vrankrijk, Bario, or Buka for example.

Work/office
This could be a great place, when attention is paid to the flourishing of its employees. Things can be otherwise very difficult, especially in the absence of good policy.

**School
(PO/SO/HO)**
This is not a nice place for many trans people, because of bullying and teachers who do not intervene. If there is an active GSA (Gender and Sexuality Alliance) it is often a lot safer.

**Winkels
*(supermarkets, clothing stores)***
You will find mostly young and inexperienced staff here. On the one hand you are anonymous, on the other hand customers or staff can behave very negatively because you are seen as different.

Police
The police still do not understand what equal treatment is and what equality means. Many trans people have bad experiences, all the more so depending on how marginalised your position is. The LGBT liaison Roze in Blauw (Pink in Blue) are understaffed, and they often do not yet understand the intersecting of experiences, such as being trans and black and undocumented.

The Park
Parks are often safe as public spaces, but as queer or trans you sometimes face higher risks.

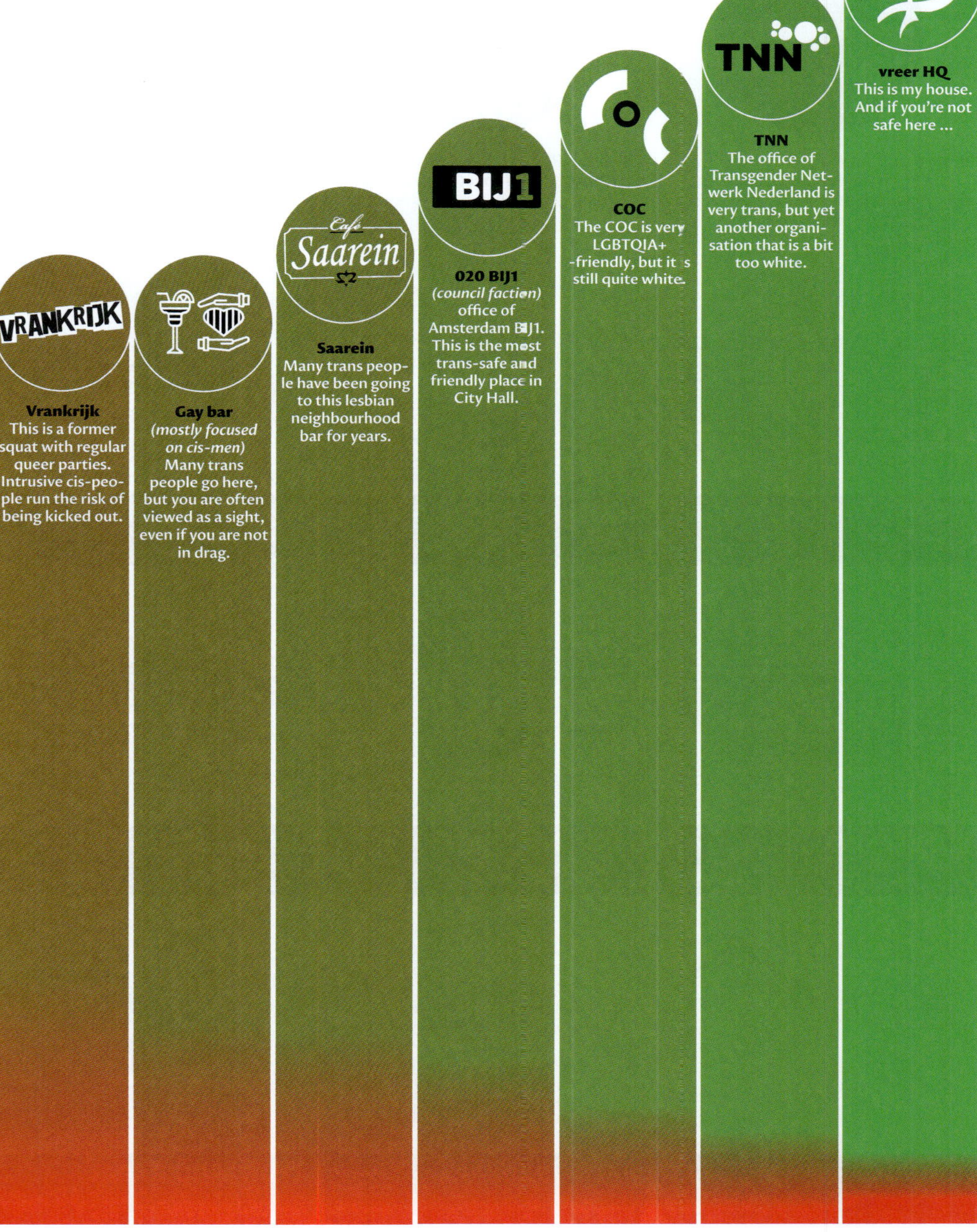
VRANKRIJK

Vrankrijk
This is a former squat with regular queer parties. Intrusive cis-people run the risk of being kicked out.

Gay bar
(mostly focused on cis-men)
Many trans people go here, but you are often viewed as a sight, even if you are not in drag.

Café Saarein

Saarein
Many trans people have been going to this lesbian neighbourhood bar for years.

BIJ1

020 BIJ1
(council faction) office of Amsterdam BIJ1. This is the most trans-safe and friendly place in City Hall.

COC
The COC is very LGBTQIA+ -friendly, but it's still quite white.

TNN

TNN
The office of Transgender Netwerk Nederland is very trans, but yet another organisation that is a bit too white.

vreer HQ
This is my house. And if you're not safe here …

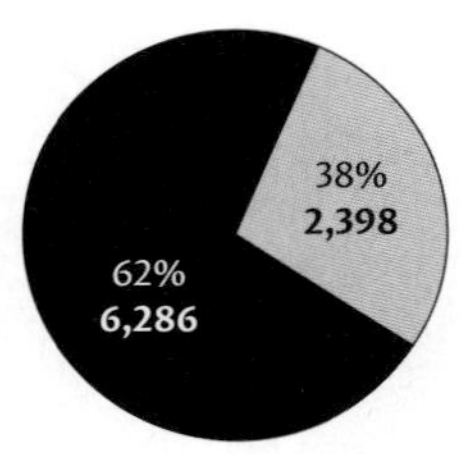

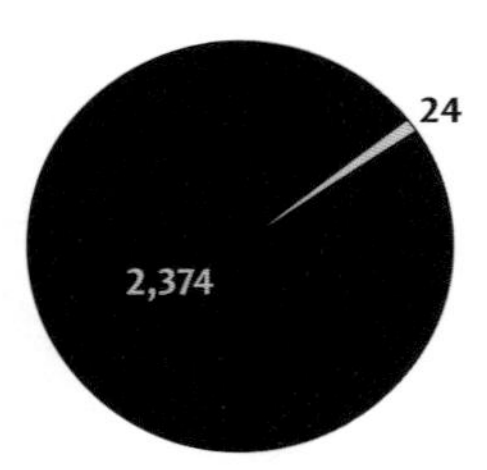

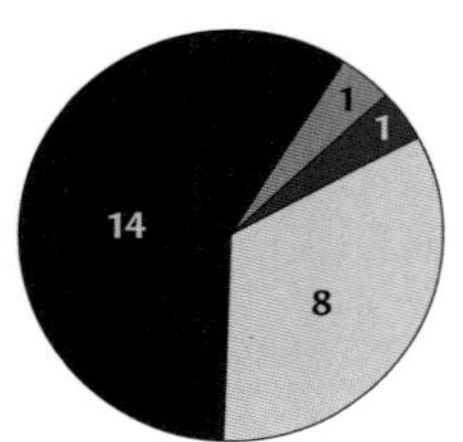

Of the 6,286 streets in Amsterdam, 38% (2,398) are named after one person. The other 62% are named after places, objects, events, and activities.

Of the 2,398 street names, twenty-four are named after suspected LGBI persons, eight after bridges, and sixteen after streets.

In total, as far as we know, fourteen gay men are named, eight lesbians, one intersexual person, and one bisexual person. The 'T' of trans is absent.

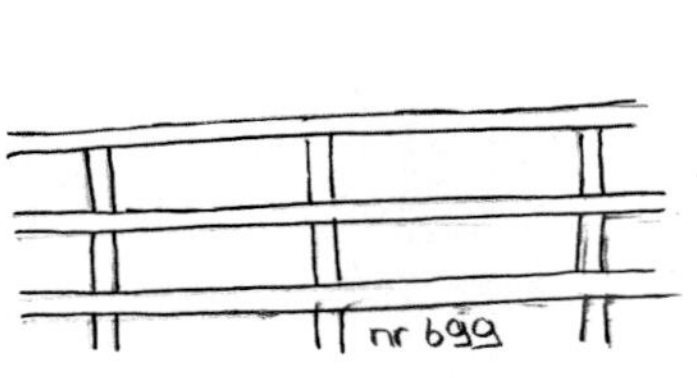

MICHEL FOUCAULTBRUG
SLOTERMEER

LOUIS COUPERUS STRAAT
SLOTERMEER

WIM SONNEVELD BRUG
CENTRUM

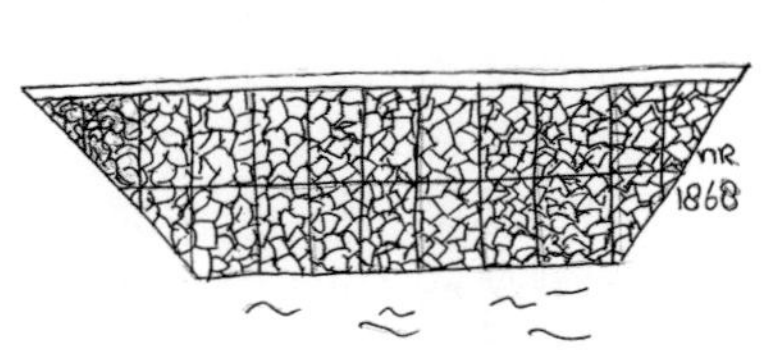

PIA BECKBRUG
SLOTERVAART

BOUTENSSTRAAT
SLOTERMEER

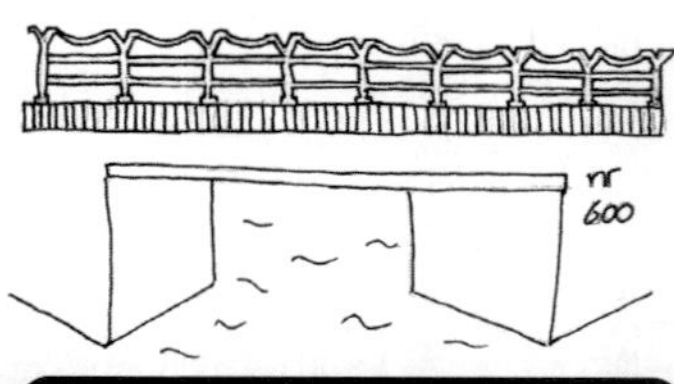

FRIEDA BELINFANTEBRUG
NIEUW WEST

ARONDEUSSTRAAT
SLOTERMEER

BALDWINSTRAAT
OSDORP

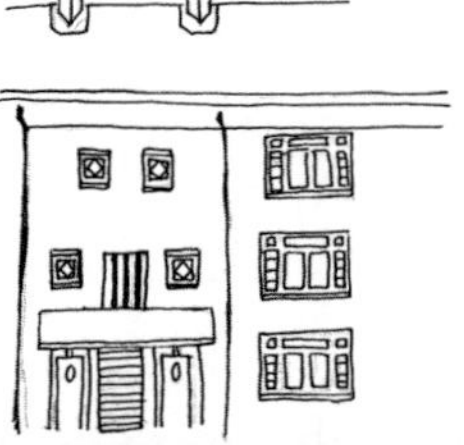

LEONARDOSTRAAT
ZUID

—under construction—

LEEN JONGEWAARD KADE
NOORD

ALBERT MOLHOF
NOORD

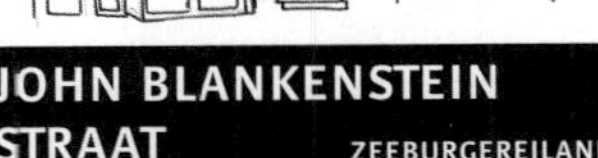

ALAN TURINGPLEIN
WATERGRAAFSMEER

TOLLIEN SCHUURMAN BRUG
ZEEBURGEREILAND

JOHN BLANKENSTEIN STRAAT
ZEEBURGEREILAND

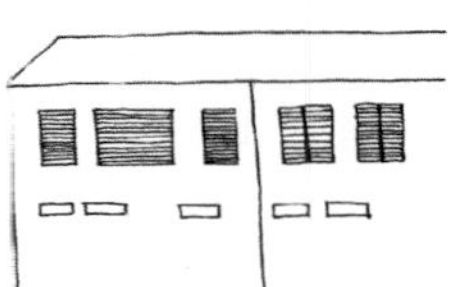

BET VAN BEERENBRUG
CENTRUM

JACOB ISRAËL DE HAAN STRAAT
DE PIJP

FOEKJE DILLEMASTRAAT
ZEEBURGEREILAND

GERARD REVE BRUG
DE PIJP / RIVIERENBUURG

HENRIËTTE BOSMANS STRAAT
ZUID

MARGUERITE YOURCENAR STRAAT
BIJLMERMEER

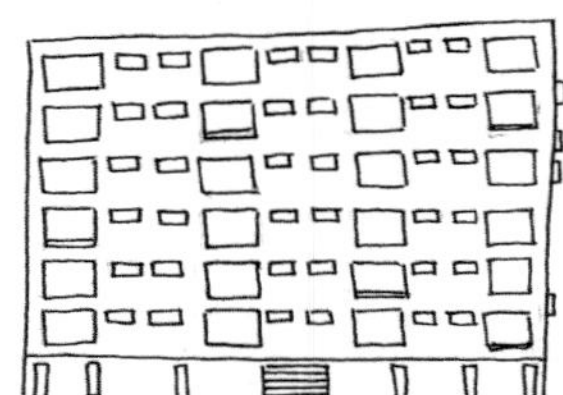

ANNA VOCKSTRAAT
BIJLMERMEER

EDITH MAGNUS STRAAT
BIJLMERMEER

ANNA BLAMANSINGEL
VENSTERPOLDER

As in any big city, local entrepreneurs give neighbourhoods their character. Everywhere in Noord you will find people that have been refusing to surrender to the power of corporations. Lone wolves, small entrepreneurs, and family businesses who are committed with heart and soul. They don't just make money; they make culture.

Ellen from doll shop 'Colourful Goodies', Van der Pekstraat 75 HS

Roos from laundry service 'De Roos', Van der Pekstraat 55/57

Oussi from Snack bar ''t Puntje', Buikslotermeerplein 160

Mahmud from Coffeeshop 'Atlas', Parlevinker 8

Abdellah from fish shop 'Al Hoceima', Waddenweg 9

Erik & Ingrid from hardware shop 'Burger & Zn IJzerwaren', Meeuwenlaan 315

Gerrie & Els from flower service 'Zwaan', Het Laagt 701

Ibo from 'Ibo's' Traiteur and Catering', Purmerplein 22

Once upon a time, to live in a little place in the Jordaan neighbourhood only cost seven guilders a month. Those times are long gone, but if you take a closer look, you will find the older residents who have managed to survive, against all odds of gentrification. What are their life lessons?

Hennie (68) has been living in the Jordaan all her life.
'What goes around, comes around.'

Herman (71) has been co-owner of the 'Hermanusje van alles' drugstore in the Jordaan for forty-seven years.
He used to live there but is now living in Purmerend. 'Fresh air is the best medicine.'

Rikie (77) was born in the Jordaan, then moved to Amsterdam Zuid, and is now living in the Jordaan again.
'A good neighbour is worth more than a distant friend.'

Rooie Anne (79) has been living in the Jordaan all her life.
'There is no point in comparing yourself to others.'

Marijke (80) grew up on the canals and is now living in the Jordaan.
'Think for yourself.'

Annie (83) has been living in the Jordaan all her life.
'Everybody sings to their own tune.'

Stanley (86) was born in Suriname, grew up in De Pijp, and is now living in the Jordaan.
'Family is everything.'

Ernst (89) lived in the Jordaan all his life, but moved to Purmerend a year ago.
'Everyone should be able to make ends meet.'

Ripple Effect
Natascha Hagenbeek in co-creation with commoners and Vincent Bogers

Welcome Stranger
Nickisch Holger

EuroPride Amsterdam 1994
Vincent van der Kaap

Sweet and Breakable
Anastasia Campbell

mOOKum
Sytse de Maat

A Caring Metropole
Maarten van Asbeck

Krijgen we het nog op een rijtje?
Geert Mol

My Amsterdam
Sieto van der Scheer

Together is Better
Mathilde muPe

Controlled
Anonymous

Maneki-neko of Amsterdam
Minhong Yu

Heldhaftig, vastberaden, barmhartig
Wouter Stroet

Amsterdamned
Julina Bezold

Priority
Annelys de Vet

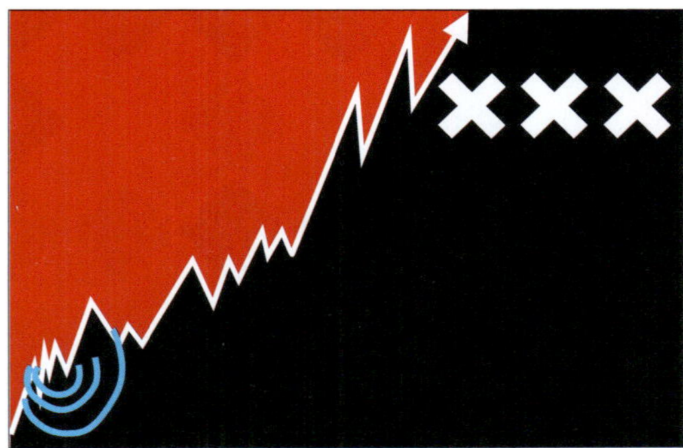

For the Rich?
Anne Vera Veen

Golden Ratio
Tatyana Dmitrieva

My Amsterdam, My Choice
Zjef van Bezouw

Nexus Connection
Victor van Zanten

Mirror
Tatyana Dmitrieva

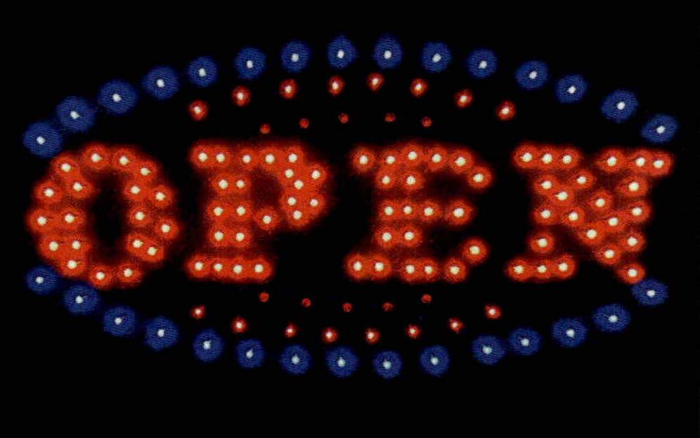

Openness
Minhong Yu

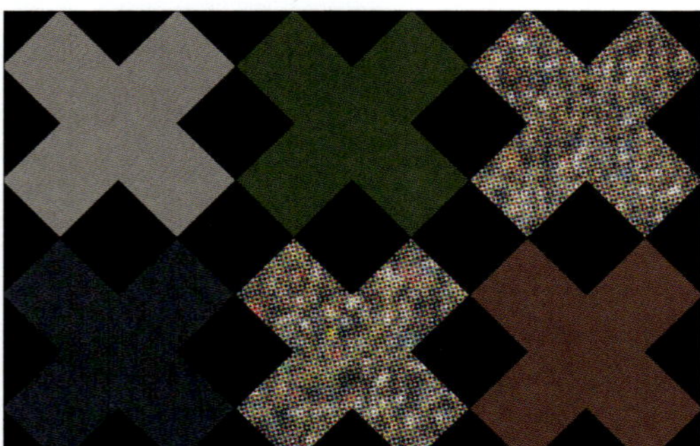

People Nature Buildings
Bence Török

Colours
Bence Török

Straight Up
Geke Oosterhof

12m² / €1200
Anne Vera Veen

Free Amsterdam
Hans Smit

Goddess of Connection
Toon Jansen

Power of Diversity
Rosemarie van Dijk

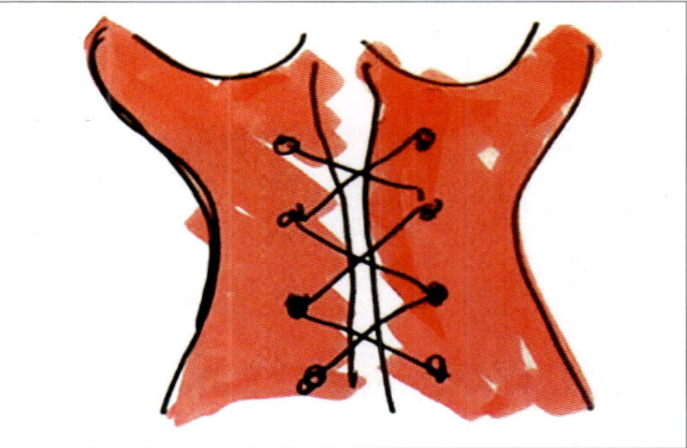

Feminine, Cheerful, and Bold!
Liesbeth van der Pol

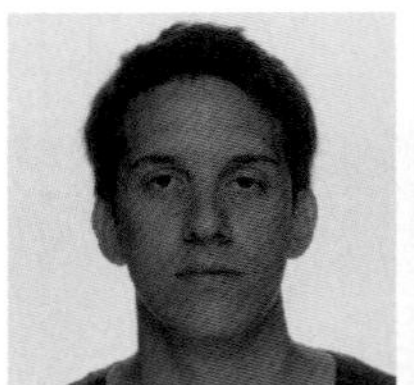

Deniz Aktaş, *Oud West (1994, Istanbul, TR) PhD candidate in Anthropology & Religious Studies*
p. 136

David Albilal, *Noord (1994, SY) Student Middle-Eastern studies, singer*
p. 30

Lama Aloul, *Nieuw Sloten (1997, Halhul-Hebron, PS) Designer, artist, researcher*
p. 35

Qusai Alsaify, *Bijlmer (1987, SY) Artist*
p. 110

Saja Amro, *West (1993, Bethlehem, PS) Architect*
p. 80, 110

Najah Aouaki, *Zuidoost (1979, Alphen aan de Rijn, NL) Economist and urban strategist*
p. 13

Maarten van Asbeck, *Staatsliedenbuurt (1963, Zeist, NL) Teacher, entrepreneur*
p. 172

Roumaisae Azoufri, *West (2005, Amsterdam, NL) High-school student*
p. 19

Bador, *We Sell Reality*
p. 48, 52, 120, 124

Julina Bezold, *Hoofddorpleinbuurt (1992, Essen, DE) Body designer*
p. 122, 173

Zjef van Bezouw, *Centrum (1960, Gilzen en Rijen, NL) Creative director*
p. 174

Ravi Blits, *Centrum (1998, Amsterdam, NL) Tinkerer*
p. 42

Eva Bollen, *Noord, Vogele buurt (1966, Amsterdam, NL) Founder of Red Amsterdam Noord*
p. 90

Isa van Bossé, *Noord (1983, Amsterdam Zuidoost, Frissenstein, NL) Resident advisor, creative consultant*
p. 90, 154

Sam Broekman, *de Pijp (1996, Arnhem, NL) Cinematographer*
p. 104, 162

Eeke Brussee, *Leiden (1998, Oranjestad, Aruba) Cultural Anthropologist, sociologist*
p. 112

Nell Bucher, *Oost, Science Park, Indische buurt (2000, Paris, FR) Filmmaker*
p. 37

Anastasia Campbell, *Kadijken (1999, Dubai, UAE) Political Science & Heritage and Memory Studies*
p. 171

Piotr Chmielewski, *Bos en Lommer (1994, Warsaw, PL) Historian*
p. 126

Rasha Dakkak, *Slotervaart (1990, Abu Dhabi, UAE) Designer*
p. 80

Joséphine Dupuy d'Angeac, *Spaarndammerbuurt (1996, Paris 15ième, FR) Activist* **p. 116**

Moussa Dembele, *Noord (1992, Ivoorkust, CI) Elderly care worker (Cordaan)* **p. 34**

Roos van Dijk, *Westelijke Eilanden (1979, Alkmaar, NL) City of Amsterdam, BIA* **p. 175**

Maria Dijkgraaf, *Noord (1994, Meppel, NL) Studiecoördinator, cellist* **p. 66**

Tatyana Dmitrieva, *Diemen (1988, Novosibirsk, RU) Artist* **p. 173, 174**

Robbie Doorman, *Tuindorp Oostzaan (1996, Den Haag, NL) Artist* **p. 88**

Janfrans van der Eerden, *GWL-terrein (Zuid Holland, NL) Architect, teacher* **p. 38**

Eid, *We Sell Reality* **p. 30, 48, 120, 124**

Idris Elhassan, *Volewijck (1983, London, UK) Engineer, artist* **p. 138**

Elke *We Sell Reality* **p. 16, 48, 120, 124**

Farah Fayyad, *De Pijp (1990, Beirut, LB) Graphic designer, printmaker* **p. 110**

Maxime Garcia Diaz, *Noord (1993, Amsterdam, NL) Poet* **p. 104**

Layla Gijsen, *Jordaan (1999, Amsterdam Prinseneiland, NL) Student Gerrit Rietveld Academie* **p. 94**

Merna Gomaa, *Geuzenveld (2006, Alexandrië, EG) High-school student* **p. 21**

Eric Groot Kormelink, *Oud-Zuid (1972, Winterswijk, NL) Policy officer accessibility and mobility* **p. 96**

Natascha Hagenbeek, *Landsmeer (1970, Leusden, NL) Artist* **p. 170**

Hamo, *We Sell Reality* **p. 48, 120, 124**

Ayman Hassan, *Centrum (1990, Limassol, CY) Graphic designer* **p. 45, 110**

Hayat, *We Sell Reality* **p. 17, 48, 120, 124**

Nickisch Holger, *Staatsliedenbuurt (1963, Gelsenkirchen, DE) Artist, curator for mostly public spaces* **p. 170**

Lucas Huikeshoven, *Noord*
(1997, Amsterdam, NL)
Artist, filmmaker
p. 162

Toon Jansen, *Houthavens*
Writer, painter
p. 175

Vincent van der Kaap,
Centrum (1964)
Tailor, educator
p. 171

Chris Keulemans, *Noord*
(1960, Tunis, TN)
Author
p. 86

Indira van 't Klooster,
Zaandam (1971, Utrecht,
NL) *Director, Amsterdam
Architecture Centre (Arcam)*
p. 6, 182

Kees de Klein, *Noord*
(1988, Nijmegen, NL)
Designer
p. 46

Sadali Koralege, *Noord,
NDSM* (2005, Amsterdam,
NL) *High-school student*
p. 40

Siwar Kraitem, *Slotervaart*
(1992, Beirut, LB)
Designer, artist
p. 130

Adinda van Kranendonk,
Noord (1991, Zutphen, NL)
Anthropologist
p. 142

Darko Lagunas, *Jordaan*
(1987, Amsterdam, NL)
*Environmental sociologist,
immersive ethnographic
fieldwork*
p. 102

Tara Lane, *Leicestershire*
(2007, Leicestershire, UK)
High school student
p. 20

Tina Lenz, *Noord*
(1972, Alkmaar, NL)
Design anthropologist
p. 148

Sytse de Maat, *Oostelijk
Havengebied* (1963, Breda,
NL) *Architect*
p. 172

Mahmoud,
We Sell Reality
p. 32, 48, 120, 124

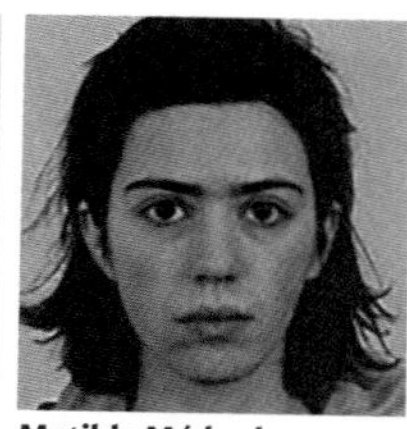

Matilda Médard,
Gentiaanbuurt (1996,
Chatenay, Malabry, FR)
*Filmmaker, painter, member
of Radio Voorwaarts*
p. 92

Yannesh Meijman,
Westerpark
(1995, Amsterdam, NL)
Filmmaker
p. 53

Stefan Meyer, *De Bijlmer*
(1992, Ingolstadt, DE)
Artist, architect
p. 68

Ott Metusala, *De Wallen*
(1988, Tallinn, EE)
Designer
p. 110

Mohamed,
We Sell Reality
p. 48, 120, 124

Lou de Monchy, *Oostelijk
Havengebied* (1996,
Amsterdam, NL)
*Masterstudent ASCA,
activist*
p. 136

Geert Mol, *Aker*
(1960, Amsterdam, NL)
Architect
p. 172

Mathilde muPe, *Centrum*
(1962, Amsterdam,NL)
Artist
p. 172

Nasra,
We Sell Reality
p. 48, 120, 124

Naira Nigrelli, *Amsterdam West* (1996, Milaan, IT)
Cultural worker
p. 106

Geke Oosterhof, *Indische Buurt* (1960, Hellendoorn, NL) *Cultural entrepeneur*
p. 175

Wouter Pocornie, *Zuid-oost* (1986, Amsterdam, NL)
Architect, urban planner, researcher
p. 56, 182

Liesbeth van der Pol, *Oosterparkbuurt*
(1959, Amsterdam, NL)
Architect
p. 175

Paandyar Pourseyf, *Geuzenveld* (2004, Amsterdam, NL)
High-school student
p. 41

Mars Remijn, *Zuidoost* (2001, Voorschoten, NL)
Student of Musicology
p. 39

Laura van Roemburg, *Noord* (1989, Amsterdam, NL) *Curator, photo editor*
p. 108

Alexandra Rouppe van der Voort, *de Baarsjes*
(1968, Den Bosch, NL)
Visual artist
p. 74, 146

Sarah Saleh, *De Pijp*
(1996, Beirut, LB)
Sound designer
p. 44

Sami,
We Sell Reality
p. 48, 120, 124

Nadia Sbai, *Slotervaart*
(1977, Nador, MA)
Activity support
p. 148

Sieto van der Scheer, *Jordaan* (1969, IJsselmuiden, NL) *Designer, architect*
p. 172

Rob Schröder, *Centre*
(1950, Oegstgeest, NL)
Designer, filmmaker, activist
p. 76

Hans Smit, *Aker*
(1950, Amsterdam, NL)
p. 175

Shadi Srewel, *Noord*
(1991, SY) *Architect*
p. 31

Gijs Stork, *Centre* (1964, Amsterdam, NL) *Curator*
p. 18

Robin Stark,
Gentiaanbuurt
(1995, Amsterdam, NL)
Bartender
p. 82

Annelys de Vet, *previously Oud-Zuid (1974, Alkmaar, NL) Designer, researcher, educator*
p. 6, 11, 173, 182, 184, 188

Minhong Yu, *Staatsliedenn buurt – Amsterdam West (1990, Dalian, CN) Visual designer, artist, curator in-between West and East*
p. 134, 173

Iriée Zamblé, *Rotterdam (1995, Amsterdam, NL) Artist*
p. 152

Victor van Zanten, *Centrum (1941, Holland, NL) All-over design*
p. 174

Juha van 't Zelfde, *Noord, Nieuwendam (1979, Zeist, NL) Artist, organiser*
p. 72

Hans de Zwart, *Staatsliedenbuurt (1976) Teacher, researcher, activist*
p. 50

COLLECTIVES

Failed Architecture, *a platform for spatial criticism, reconnecting architecture with the real world*
p. 46

Hotel Mokum, *a squatting collective*
p. 117, 118

Team Zuidoost
Lead by Wouter Pocornie | Bijlmer Believers 3.0 (Bijlm3r) In collaboration with: Vesla Braafheid, Menny Things, and Bartendaz, with support from Kazerne Reigersbos, Hart voor de K-buurt, Swazoom, and local residents
p. 26, 56, 60, 62, 182

Verdedig Noord, *an activist group grappling with the gentrification of Amsterdam Noord*
p. 78, 182, 187

We Sell Reality, *a social art collective*
p. 48, 120, 124, 182, 185

Architectuur Centrum Amsterdam
Director: Indira van 't Klooster
Project coordinator: Anne Vera Veen

Subjective Editions
Editor-in-chief: Annelys de Vet
Publisher: Kurt Vanbelleghem

Support
Financially supported by: AFK,
Stimuleringsfonds Creatieve Industrie,
and supported by housing corporation Ymere

Graphic designer
Wouter Stroet supports all workshops and ensures
coherent visual output in dialogue with the
authors.

Partners
Seven representatives of organisations, each
initiating a workshop and inviting visual authors:
Verdedig Noord, We Sell Reality, Team Zuidoost,
IHLIA, Startblok Elzenhagen, Radio Voorwaarts,
Sandberg Instituut (Disarming Design)

Radio Voorwaarts
Radio Voorwaarts is a collective for the arts,
counterculture, and activism—deeply rooted
in Amsterdam. Especially now that such a large
monoculture prevails in the city, Radio Voorwaarts
is trying to present itself by offering autonomous
space for cultural makers who are gradually
experiencing less of it in the city.

We Sell Reality
We Sell Reality is a social art collective consisting of
ten designers and artists. Their work mainly consists
of products, public installations, and performances.
Almost everyone in the group arrived as a refugee
and still does not have the necessary documents to
be able to officially call themselves a Dutch citizen.

Sandberg Instituut, Disarming Design
Disarming Design was a two-year temporary
master's programme committed to design
practices that deal with conditions of conflict,
oppressive forces, and entangled histories. It
hosted seventeen designers and artists hailing
from various backgrounds, all living in Amsterdam
for the period of their study, many of them in
student housing.

IHLIA
IHLIA is a heritage organisation that shows
people the history of the LGBTQIA+ community.
This way, IHLIA contributes to the social
acceptance of LGBTQIA+ people today
and tomorrow.

Bijlmer Believers 3.0
Wouter Pocornie works under the name BIJLMER
BELIEVERS 3.0 on a philosophical foundation for
spatial strategies in Amsterdam Zuidoost. It is a
creative, productive initiative determined to make
the future Zuidoost shine. Vesla Braafheid, Menny
Things, and Bartendaz have joined the *Subjective
Atlas* project and Kazerne Reigersbos, Hart voor de
K-buurt, Swazoom, and some local residents have
supported various working sessions and provided
the project with resources.

Verdedig Noord
Actiegroep (action group) Verdedig Noord consists
of people who are committed to grappling with the
gentrification of Amsterdam Noord through art,
activism, and campaigning. They want to create
awareness among old and *nieuwe Noorderlingen*
(Noord's newcomers) to improve their
relationships. In weekly meetings in the community
centre, members discuss which actions they can
take to show that changes and improvements in
Noord should not be at the expense of people who
have lived there all their lives.

Startblok Elzenhagen

Startblok Elzenhagen is a campus in Amsterdam
Noord where young Dutch people and young
status holders who have just received a residence
permit live together. A total of 540 young people
share a corridor and a common living room, spread
over different buildings and floors. Everyone lives
in the same unit of twenty-five square metres,
including a private bathroom and kitchenette.

Visual Authors

Visual authors map a place from their
own experience. They are invited
by the parnters and editors of this atlas.

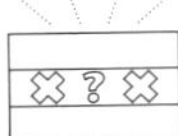

Open Call

Open call to contribute alternative flags
for Amsterdam.

Author Introduction

Najah Aouaki

Creative Commons

Published under Creative Commons
Attribution-Noncommercial-NoDerivatives 4.0
International-licentie (CC BY-NC-ND 4.0).

aMsterdam

A diverse city where the architecture debate
can become more inclusive, broader,
and taken out of the exclusive domain of 'experts'.

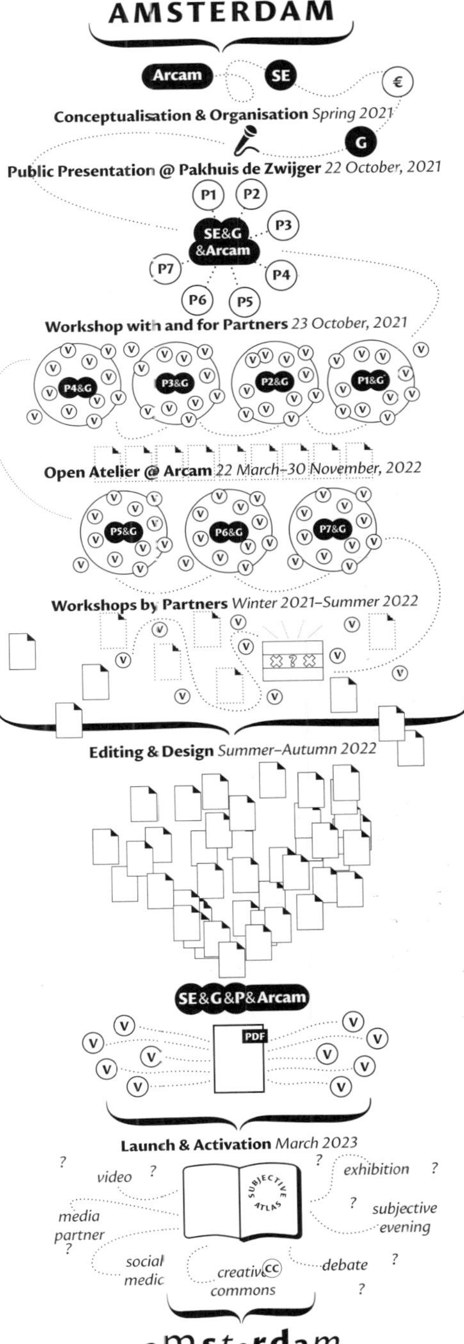

Conceptualisation & Organisation, *Spring 2021*
By June 2021, it is clear that Arcam and Subjective Editions would collaborate in developing the *Subjective Atlas of Amsterdam*, with support from various (€) funds . We engage a (G) graphic designer and invite seven (P) partners.

Kick-off, *Pakhuis de Zwijger, 22 October, 2021*
The project officially opens with an evening event at Pakhuis de Zwijger, where the (SE) *Subjective Atlas of Amsterdam* and its motivations are shared with the general public.

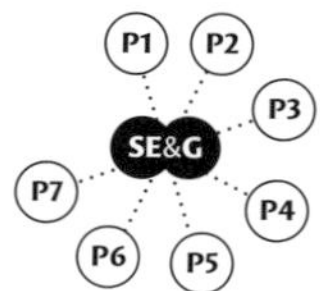

Workshop with and for Partners
Arcam, 23 October, 2021
We collaborate with seven (P) partner organisations, who will invite people from their own networks to contribute to the (SE) Atlas. The

coordinators of these seven partner organisations assemble in a master workshop, supervised by Annelys de Vet (Subjective Editions' designer and editor-in-chief), developing the very first contributions, discussing the concept and methodology, and establishing the practicalities.

Photo: Sanne Couprie

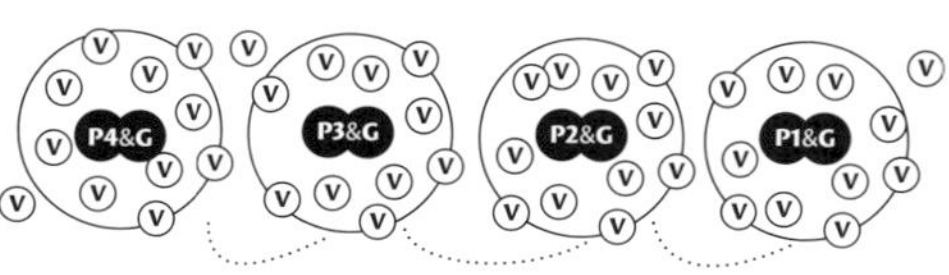

Workshops by Partners, *2021–2022*
Between November 2021 and August 2022, each (P) partner organises a working session at their own location, inviting participants from their network. The working sessions usually have the same structure: in the morning, everyone is welcomed by the host at their location, and they begin with a round of introductions. Everyone talks about their morning, in order to start reflecting on their daily routines from a subjective position. Anne Vera Veen (Arcam) (Arcam, visual anthropologist and project coordinator) and Wouter Stroet (G) (artist and graphic designer) make a presentation about the project. After a meal, the participants set to work

on their contributions. Using sketch paper, comput-
ers, photos, and by exchanging information, each
participant reflects on their subjective experience of
Amsterdam. The participants will develop their contributions for some weeks after the working session.

P1&G

Radio Voorwaarts, *Vrankrijk, 8 December, 2021*

P2&G

We Sell Reality, *FramerFramed, 17 December, 2021*

P2&G

Disarming Design, Sandberg Instituut,
Fabulous Future, 10 February, 2022

P4&G

IHLIA, *OBA (Amsterdam Public Library),*
5 April, 2022

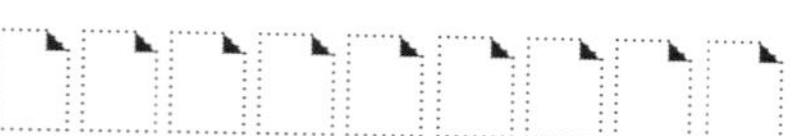

Open Atelier,

Arcam, 22 March–30 November, 2022
Incoming contributions are being exhibited at the
Open Atelier, an interactive exhibition at **Arcam**
Arcam. Visitors are invited to draw their own subjective map and to hang them between the other
visual contributions on display. The exhibition has
a grand opening in April, featuring presentations of
several ⓥ creators.

The insights we gain and topics that surface during the first few workshops shape the sessions that follow.

P5&G

Kids Zuidoost, *Arcam, 26 April, 2022*
Bijlmer Believers 3.0, *Zuidoost, April-May 2022*

P6&G

Verdedig Noord, *Buurthuis de Rietwijker, 12 May, 2022*

P7&G

Startblok Elzenhagen
Startblok Elzenhagen, 10 July, 2022

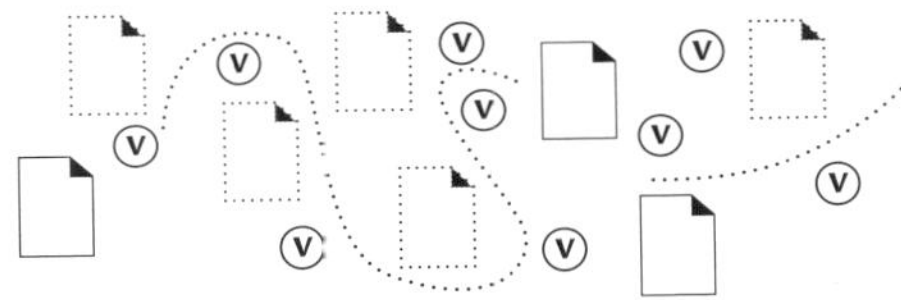

Editing & Design *Summer–Autumn 2022*
During an editorial meeting, we **SE&G&P&Arcam** reflect on the contributions we collected and think about the perspectives that are most clearly missing. Based on this observation, we invite a few individuals whose perspective is complementary to the contributions already received.

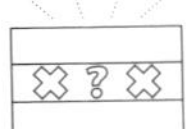

Open Call, *Autumn 2022*
Through an open call, we collect alternative flags of Amsterdam.

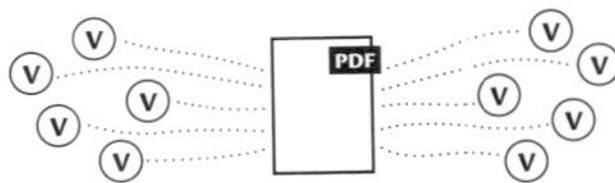

Final Check, *Winter 2022*
Before the publication goes to the printer, all those involved provide feedback on the draft document.

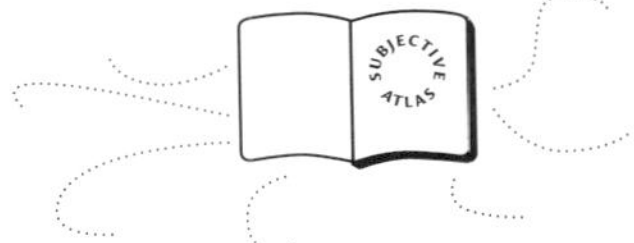

Book launch & Activation,
Pakhuis de Zwijger, March 2023
During the book launch at Pakhuis de Zwijger, several authors discuss the creative process and their contribution to the *Subjective Atlas*.

Subjective Atlases are bottom-up, cartographic publications mapping a country, region, or city by the inhabitants themselves. The atlases offer an emotional geography of lived experiences that opens up political scopes, contributing to a more pluralistic and sensitive territorial identification.

Subjective Editions is the publishing platform that develops participative production processes and distributes the engaged publications. We support communities in mapping their environments from the inside out, starting from a place-based understanding, and grounded in lived experiences. We explore the individual in relation to the collective, the subjective in relation to the apparently objective, the personal in relation to the political.

Method

We work on the basis of ① invitations by local partners with whom we co-develop a mapping trajectory. ② Over several workshops, inhabitants of a place are invited to participate in the mapping process by creating a visual representation of what that region personally means to them. ③ Together with the local partner we coordinate the editing, designing, ④ printing, publishing, and distribution ⑤ process of their edition of the *Subjective Atlas*.

The project offers a platform for collective visual dialogue to challenge social, political, and cultural circumstances of our day-to-day realities. ⑥ The bottom-up approach questions dominant ways of representing territories and demystifies map-making itself.

Organisation

Since 2018, Subjective Editions is registered as a Belgian non-profit organisation (vzw), with a studio near Brussels and a team operating internationally. For each Atlas, we work with local partners and international distributors. Our core team currently consists of Annelys de Vet (founder & editor-in-chief) and Kurt Vanbelleghem (producer & publisher).

www.subjectiveeditions.org

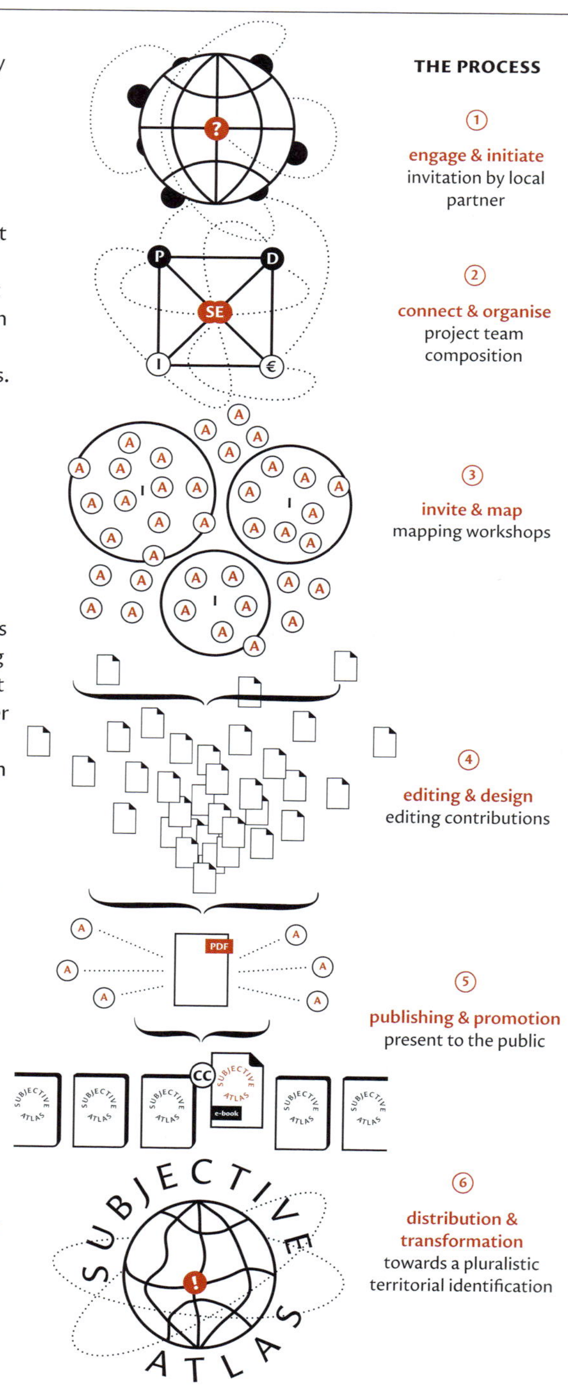

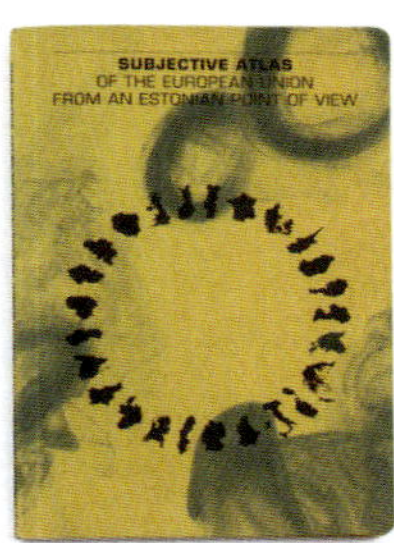

Subjective Atlas of the EU
2003. EN
A. de Vet, K. Mändmaa (ed.)
& Estonian School of Arts

Subjectieve Atlas van Nederland
BIS Publishers, 2005. NL
A. de Vet (ed.)
& Design Academy Eindhoven

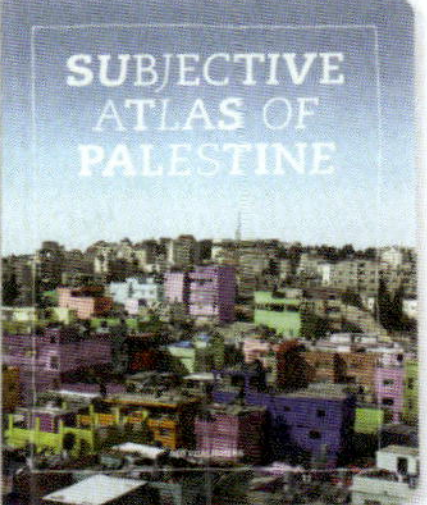

Subjective Atlas of Palestine
010 Publishers, 2007. EN
K. Hourani, A. de Vet (ed.)
& International Academy of Arts Palestine

Subjective Atlas of Serbia
Dom Omladine, 2009. EN
M. Kovac, A. de Vet (ed.)
& Dom Omladine

Subjective Atlas of Hungary
HVG Könyvek & Kitchen Budapest , 2011.
EN-HU. A. Bujdoso, A. de Vet (ed.)
& Kitchen Budapest

Subjective Atlas of Mexico
LAST, 2011. EN-ES
M. Driesse, A. Sclomonoff, A. de Vet
(ed.) & Casa Vecina, Ule, Iago and Aavi

Subjective Atlas of Fryslân
Afuk, 2013. NL-FRY–EN
R. Koster, A. de Vet (ed.)
& Keunstwurk, Academie voor Popcultuur

Subjective Atlas of Hainaut
Grand-Hornu Images, 2013. FR-EN
M. Driesse, A. de Vet (ed.) & Grand-
Hornu Images, Fédération du Tourisme

Subjective Atlas of Colombia
Semana Libros, 2015. EN-ES
M. Driesse, H.H. Tobón, A. de Vet (ed.) &
Universidad de los Andes, La Usurpadora

Subjective Atlas of Pakistan
Subjective Editions, 2018. EN
T. Shaheen, A. de Vet (ed.)
& University of Karachi

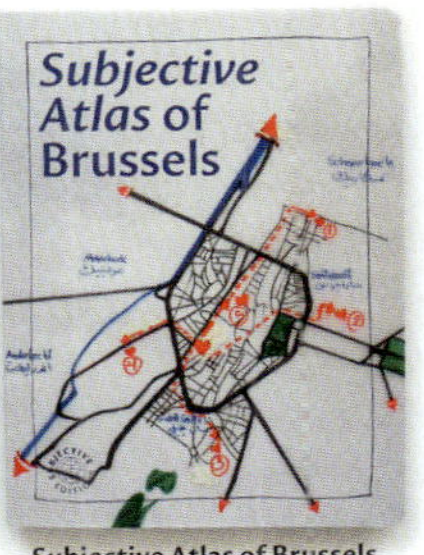

Subjective Atlas of Brussels
Subjective Editions, 2018. EN
A. de Vet (ed.) & MAD Brussels,
Globe Aroma, Academie Anderlecht

Subjective Atlas of Luxembourg
Subjective Editions, 2018. EN
A. de Vet (ed.)
& Casino, forum d'art contemporain

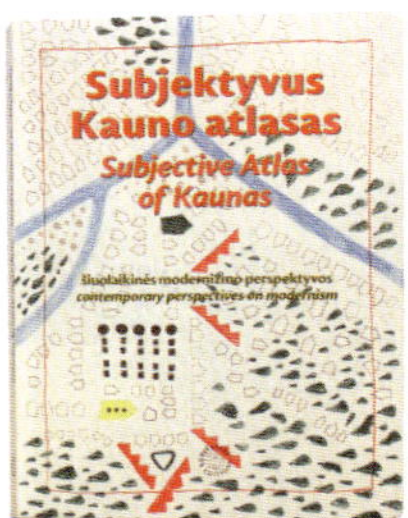

Subjective Atlas of Kaunas
Subjective Editions, 2022. LT-EN
H.H. Hobón (ed.)
& Kaunas2022

Subjective Atlas of Amsterdam
Subjective Editions, 2023. EN
W. Stroet, A. Veen,
A. de Vet (ed.) & Arcam

For thirty-five years, Arcam has been the central point for architecture in Amsterdam—a meeting place for anyone interested in architecture, urban planning, landscape design, and their own role in shaping Amsterdam's living environment. Arcam highlights and explores current urban challenges and ambitions. In doing so, Arcam looks at the role that designers, policymakers, contractors, clients, and the public can play in shaping the urban environment, offering an independent and diverse platform through which they can have their say.

Arcam's regular programme consists of exhibitions, talks, walks, guided tours, and publications. Arcam is serving the design community by providing the opportunity to reflect on and debate major design challenges in the Amsterdam region within a global context, by offering an educational programme, by helping tourists on their way to new architectural hotspots, by informing interested parties about urban development, and by listening to users and Amsterdam residents, facilitating their feedback to the design community.

Through its programmes, Arcam wants to do right by all stories, identities, and cultures that Amsterdam is home to. In doing so, Arcam takes into account differences in culture, gender, age, physical limitations, level of education, and the coexistence of human and nature in and around the city. Arcam involves a diverse audience in the city's design assignments and in discussions about Amsterdam's architecture. Arcam's programs are accessible but critical—conscious of history, but always keeping an eye on the future.

Arcam
Prins Hendrikkade 600
1011 VX Amsterdam
the Netherlands
www.arcam.nl

ar c am

The building, designed by architect René van Zuuk, where Arcam is housed

Located at the Prins Hendrikkade in Amsterdam, Arcam takes a central position in the city that is the subject of its programme

View of the exhibition *Private_Eye_Butler_Spy March–June 2022*

Arcam's exhibitions attempt to stir interaction and reflection

COLOPHON

This publication is a result of a collaboration between Subjective Editions and Arcam

Editor-in-Chief
Annelys de Vet (Subjective Editions)

Research, Development, and Editing
Anne Vera Veen (Arcam), Wouter Stroet

Introductions
Najah Aouaki, Indira van 't Klooster, Anne Vera Veen, Annelys de Vet

Contributors
Deniz Aktaş, David Albilal, Lama Aloul, Qusai Alsaify, Saja Amro, Najah Aouaki, Maarten van Asbeck, Roumaisae Azoufri, Bador, Julina Bezold, Zjef van Bezouw, Ravi Blits, Eva Bollen, Isa van Bossé, Sam Broekman, Eeke Brussee, Nell Bucher, Anastasia Campbell, Piotr Chmielewski, Rasha Dakkak, Joséphine Dupuy d'Angeac, Moussa Dembele, Rosemarie van Dijk, Maria Dijkgraaf, Tatyana Dmitrieva, Robbie Doorman, Janfrans van der Eerden, Eid, Idris Elhassan, Farah Fayyad, Maxime Garcia Diaz, Layla Gijsen, Eric Groot Kormelink, Natascha Hagenbeek, Hamo, Ayman Hassan, Hayat, Nickisch Holger, Lucas Huikeshoven, Toon Jansen, Vincent van der Kaap, Chris Keulemans, Indira van 't Klooster, Kees de Klein, Sadali Koralege, Siwar Kraitem, Adinda van Kranendonk, Darko Lagunas, Tara Lane, Tina Lenz, Sytse de Maat, Mahmoud, Matilda Médard, Yannesh Meijman, Stefan Meyer, Ott Metusala, Mohamed, Lou de Monchy, Geert Mol, Mathilde muPe, Nasra, Naira Nigrelli, Geke Oosterhof, Wouter Pocornie, Liesbeth van der Pol, Paandyar Pourseyf, Mars Remijn, Laura van Roemburg, Alexandra Rouppe van der Voort, Sarah Saleh, Sami, Nadia Sbai, Sieto van der Scheer, Rob Schröder, Hans Smit, Shadi Srewel, Cijs Stork, Robin Stark, Marco Stroet, Wouter Stroet, Peik Suyling, Jara van Teeffelen, Teferi, Roman Tkachenko, Anna Torres, Finn van Tol, Bence Török, Hans de Tweede, Elke, Yuri Veerman, Anne Vera Veen, Lisa Veenstra, vreer verkerke, Samira Vogel, Dewi Vrenegoor, Rufus de Vries, Raffaela Wang, Mateo Vega, Hannah Veldhoen, Annelys de Vet, Minhong Yu, Iriée Zamblé, Victor van Zanten, Juha van 't Zelfde, Hans de Zwart and Bijlmer Believers 3.0 (Bijlm3r), Failed Architecture, Hotel Mokum, Verdedig Noord, We Sell Reality

Graphic Design
Wouter Stroet, Annelys de Vet

Workshop Coordinators
Robbie Doorman (Radio Voorwaarts), Elke Uitentuis (We Sell Reality), Dewi Vrenegoor (IHLIA), Julina Vanille Bezold, Anna Garcia Gomez, Saja Amro (Sandberg Instituut), Juha van 't Zelfde (Verdedig Noord), Wouter Pocornie (Team Zuidoost), Adinda van Kranendonk (Startblok Elzenhagen)

Production and Editorial Assistance
Finn van Tol, Emilie Tesh, Eeke Brussee (Arcam)
Natalia Lopez Lopez, Omar Kashmiry (Subjective Editions)

Communication
Femke Gerritsma (Arcam)

Translation NL–EN
Larae Malooly

Proofreading
Harriet Foyster

Typeface
Proza by Jasper de Waard

Cover Image
Ravi Blits

Terms and Conditions

Printer
Artoos Group

Financial support
Amsterdams Fonds voor de Kunsten
Stimuleringfonds voor de Creatieve Industrie

Support
Ymere

Publisher
Subjective Editions (Annelys de Vet, Kurt Vanbelleghem)

Distribution
www.ideabooks.nl

Contact
www.subjectiveeditions.org
info@subjectiveeditions.org

ISBN
9789464448016

ar c am

AFK amsterdams fonds voor de kunst

stimuleringsfonds creatieve industrie

Ymere